monsoonbooks

YOU'LL DIE IN SINGAPORE

Charles McCormac was born in Croydon, England, in 1915 and at the age of four went out to Malaya where his father was a planter. There he grew up, learning to speak Malay, Chinese, Tamil and Japanese, as well as his native English. He was sent to school in Australia and then, at eighteen, he joined the RAF.

In 1937 he was back in Malaya with the No.36 (Torpedo-Bomber) Squadron and flew in the old Vildebeestes as wireless operator and air-gunner. In 1939 he had a foretaste of what was to come, when the aircraft in which he was flying spun into the sea and he kept afloat for thirteen hours until picked up by a flying boat.

Having survived the war and his six-month great escape from a POW camp in Singapore though the jungles of Indonesia to Australia, Charles McCormac passed away in 1985 at the age of seventy.

Acclaim for *You'll Die in Singapore*

"An amazing story!" *Library Journal* (USA)

"This story is fascinating in the way that these hidden histories tend to be, bringing history to a personal level." *Expat* (Singapore)

"It is an amazing tale of hardship and endurance that reads like a thriller. It is hard to believe that it is a true story." *The Asian Review of Books* (Hong Kong)

YOU'LL DIE IN
SINGAPORE

Charles McCormac, DCM

monsoon

monsoonbooks

Published in 2005
by Monsoon Books Pte Ltd
52 Telok Blangah Road
#03-05 Telok Blangah House
Singapore 098829
www.monsoonbooks.com.sg

First published in 1954
by Robert Hale Limited

ISBN: 978-981-05-3015-0

Printed in Singapore

10 09 08   2 3 4 5 6 7 8 9

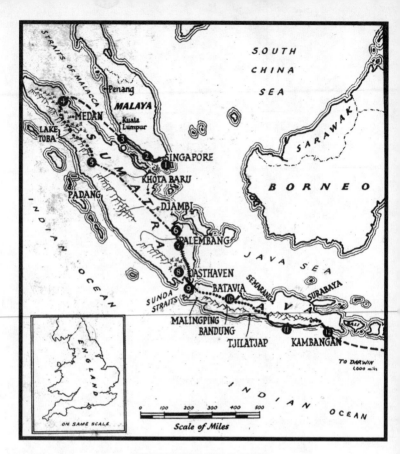

KEY TO ESCAPE ROUTE

1 Break out from Pasir Panjang
2 Machine-gunned by Japanese
3 Picked up by Dornier flying-boat
4 Starting point of jungle trek
5 By lorry with Nan Seng
6 Left Nan Seng at Palembang

7 Jumped goods train to Oasthaven
8 Worked with Eurasian road gang
9 By fishing boat to Java
10 Guerilla camp
11 By outrigger to the white *tuan*
12 Rendezvous with Catalina

• • • • • jungle trek

⁓ by boat ┼┼┼┼┼┼ by train

– – – by plane —•—•— by lorry

Foreword

After the publication of Paul Brickhill's very brief account of my escape from a Japanese prison camp on Singapore island, in his book of war stories entitled "Escape—or Die", I received many enquiries from readers who wanted to know more. Some of the questions I have been able to answer; others I haven't—partly for security reasons and partly because the events referred to have faded from memory. Mine was, after all, a hazardous experience, the important occurrences in which I shall never forget, though they have submerged the lesser important. But I hope this book will fill most of the gaps.

I take this opportunity of expressing my everlasting gratitude to those people (British, Australian, Malayan, Dutch, Sumatran, Chinese and Javanese) who played their parts in my story and without whose sacrifice I should not be alive to tell the tale. Above all, I acknowledge a great companion—that of R. G. Donaldson, the Australian who alone was with me at the end of my adventure.

Charles McCormac
Welling, Kent
September, 1954

Chapter One

Out of the pall of smoke that hung motionless above the docks of Singapore flashed a Jap fighter, sweeping low along the curve of the waterfront. Explosives shells from its twin cannon ripped into a pile of packing crates; then, like an echo to the plane's roar as it disappeared behind a half-gutted warehouse, came the crackling of flames, racing quickly through the sun-dried wood.

It was January 30th, 1942 as I stood on the blazing, bomb-pitted docks watching the *Wakefield* as slowly she stood northwestward into the Malacca Strait. Somewhere aboard her was my wife, Pat, and the fact the I would within the next few days almost certainly be captured by the Japanese seemed unimportant beside the fact that she had got away. As I watched the *Wakefield* disappear in a smother of bomb-splashes I could only pray: God protect you, Pat; you and our unborn child.

It seemed impossible to believe that only a few weeks ago Pat and I had been living quietly in the married quarters that fringed Seletar aerodrome. The war then had seemed so very far away. We enjoyed a life of ease and luxury, having little suspicion of the forces that were already undermining the structure of our way of life.

The night that ended our fool's paradise was Sunday, December 7th. We spent the evening with our friends the Dennets, in their house on the perimeter of the aerodrome. Inevitably we fell to discussing the fighting in Europe and we wondered whether the war could ever spread to the Far East. In particular we tried to analyse the strange, remote, but symptomatic atmosphere that had of late been building up between the Asiatics and the Europeans. We had the impression that the Asiatics knew more than we did about the possibilities of war in the Far East, and were already deciding on whose side they would line up. Only a few days ago the amahs had demanded, through their trade unions, a fantastic wage increase; they had, they said, to have more money because part of their wages was handed each week to the kongsis (trade unions) to pay for the war in China. But I heard from several sources that the amahs were in fact putting forward an impossible claim in the hope of being dismissed; for there was a rumour that the Japanese had threatened, when they came, to kill all natives employed by Europeans.

We discussed too the great ceremonial parade that had been held that week-end in Raffles Square. Australian troops and their impressive armour had marched and countermarched hour after hour. For the ceremonial of a single afternoon the mainland of Malaya had been almost denuded of troops.

"If the Japs want to attack us," I said, "they'll never have a better chance."

"That's it, Mac," laughed Dennet. "Tonight's the night!"

It was all something of a joke; for few of us in Singapore knew anything of the reality of war. "War will never reach us" we had always thought, and like ostriches with our heads in the sands of splendid isolation, we enjoyed our lives. At night, the clubs and restaurants were crowded with tuxedo-clad men and bare-shouldered women drifting together round the dance floors. It is true we had seen news-films of the war in Europe, the Dunkirk evacuation and the bombing of London, but the general feeling was "It can't happen here." On Seletar aerodrome life was especially good. It was reputed to be the most comfortable of all RAF stations in the Far East; it had its own golf course, its yacht club, its swimming pool and its private taxis available for all ranks at $8 (about £1) for all-day hire. The Singapore civilians accepted us with a studied tolerance, and most of the town's amenities were open to us.

The night of December 7th, 1941 put an end to all that.

I was woken by Pat. She had tossed aside the mosquito net and was tugging frantically at my shoulder.

"Darling, wake up! We're being bombed."

"Don't be silly," I muttered sleepily, "it's only thunder."

Then came a thin, high-pitched whine, developing into a crescendo shriek, like a train screaming its way out of a tunnel. Instinctively Pat dropped to the floor, and I threw myself on top of her. An explosive blast echoed around the house. We picked ourselves up and rushed to the window.

"There!" she cried. "Three of them, caught in the searchlights."

We watched the Bofors tracer spiralling lazily towards the spot-lit planes. I looked at my watch. It was 4.15 am. Towards the town of Singapore fires were burning fiercely. As I dressed hurriedly, Pat slipped into a wrap and turned on the radio. After a little while, the station at Singapore came on the air with soft dance music—but no

11

announcement.

"At any rate the radio station hasn't been hit."

I struggled into my coat, told Pat to take shelter if the aircraft returned, and made my way on to the airfield.

A bomb had flattened part of the RAF hospital, and airmen were already working in the debris. There were, they believed, no casualties. Down at the hangars, airmen were clustered together talking nervously and I heard from them the first depressing report—the forerunner of so many others—that one of our Catalinas was long overdue. Flight Sergeant Webb, a first-class pilot, and a grand crew had taken off the previous afternoon on a routine patrol; from over the Gulf of Siam he had signalled a "sighting report", after identifying Japanese shipping. His news was quickly passed on to the defence authorities but no action was taken, for the assumption was that the ships were destined for Siam. Later, when we checked on times, it became clear that the ships Webb had spotted were part of the Japanese invasion fleet that landed at Kelantan, four hundred miles north of Singapore on the east coast of Malaya. Why Webb's signal went unheeded, why Singapore was not blacked-out and why there was no reception committee awaiting the bombers, were questions that have never been answered. Webb must have been the first to know that the Japanese invasion was under way. He passed the news back and was undoubtedly shot down for his trouble. But his warning passed unheeded.

In the business centre of Singapore, which had taken most of the bombing, the "Passive Defence" services went into action with little delay. Fires were quickly extinguished and the wounded cared for with efficiency. Sixty people were killed; one hundred and thirty-three were taken to hospital.

At six o'clock that morning came the news over the Malayan radio that the British Commonwealth was at war with Japan. Our Eastern paradise was crumbling about our ears.

Next day came what was perhaps the most dispiriting news of the war. On December 5th, we at Seletar had watched with pride the magnificent spectacle of the *Prince of Wales* and the *Repulse* steaming majestically up the Johore Strait. Only a few days before, the ships had arrived at Singapore, boosting the morale of the islanders. Then they steamed away. About midday on December 9th, a Walrus aircraft landed at Seletar, and we knew by the faces of the pilot and observer that some appalling tragedy had taken place. They went straight to the Operations Room and there reported that the *Prince of Wales* and the *Repulse* had both been sunk.

Three days later Mr Duff Cooper, who was then in Singapore as chairman of the war council established there, broadcast the official news of the loss of both ships.

All this time the natives were picking up the Japanese broadcasts and boasts of success, and there soon began a sort of two-way evacuation; the Asiatics leaving the congested areas of the island and pouring over the Causeway into Johore, while the Europeans and a host of non-European refugees crowded into the island from the peninsula.

In spite of all the portents, European civilians continued to go about their business without disruption of their daily routine and without loss of confidence in the impregnability of Singapore island. But at Seletar aerodrome we soon became aware of an acute shortage of aircraft when our Catalinas started bombing attacks on land targets, and our Vildebeestes sought and found Japanese shipping.

The crews of these Vildebeestes—capable of ninety knots as against the Zeros' 250–300 mph—continued gamely with their suicidal task; but they could do little to impede the inexorable Japanese advance.

One day our commanding officer assembled the wives and families of those who were living in married quarters and told us the position about evacuation. He would have liked, he said, to get us away but could do nothing yet.

"Meanwhile, slit trenches must be dug at once," he announced. "We must hold out at all costs."

Which was, of course, a stirring and reassuring sentiment—to everyone except to Pat who, with the baby due in a couple of months, did not fancy the idea of jumping in and out of slit trenches.

Soon, visits from the Japanese bombers began to come with monotonous regularity. At first they concentrated on the aerodrome, using small anti-personnel bombs perhaps because they were anxious not to spoil a prize they knew would soon be theirs. Later, Singapore town and harbour came in for their share of the bombing, but usually the aircraft made a point of attacking Seletar on their return journey. It was all done with repetitive timing: every morning at 0950 hours and every afternoon at 1500 hours. Twenty-seven bombers flying perfect formation ... 0950 hours, 1500 hours ... day after day. In the densely populated areas in and around Singapore there were heavy casualties. Upcountry the Japanese were consolidating their landings and were spreading across and down Malaya. "Our troops have retired to prepared positions" was the daily dirge on the radio, announced with extraordinary and infuriating complacency.

Towards the end of December the situation on the Malayan front deteriorated rapidly. By December 29th, the Japs were fighting south of Ipoh; on January 2nd they landed at Kuala Selangor and by January 12th had reached Kuala Lumpur. On January 26th they were at Endau only eighty miles north of the Johore Causeway, and on the 29th they were less then twenty miles north of Seletar. The airfield was now under constant aerial bombardment and the work of the two torpedo-bomber squadrons was limited to night operations as the aircraft were not fast enough to use by day. Our losses mounted with tragic rapidity. One morning that remains especially in my memory was when two Japanese Zeros beat up the aerodrome with little opposition from the ground except the fire from the crews of the Catalinas, many of whom died in their aircraft. Hangars were set on fire and station buildings badly damaged

From the early days of the New Year, Singapore was rarely without several air raids every day. European civilians poured across the Causeway onto the island in a constant stream and by January 30th the great bulk of the British forces in the peninsula had also been withdrawn.

The island was now teeming with Europeans and Asiatics, and the casualties were frightening. Singapore was a town of bewildering contrasts. On the one hand, in the wealthy residential areas, bombing had destroyed the drains, and the stench was nauseating—the Government gave free anti-typhoid injections to everyone who applied. On the other hand, the streets in the shopping and business areas were cleaned meticulously every day and were thronged with European men and women. The labourers employed at the docks, usually in large numbers, had almost entirely disappeared and British and Indian troops had to be diverted to the loading and unloading of ships. There were no shelters; the bombers rarely met opposition from our aircraft, and the anti-aircraft fire was ineffective.

What was quite astounding was the serene confidence of the European community; they really seemed to believe the Government's announcements that Singapore was impregnable. Women from the peninsula who were living uncomfortably in billets and with no more clothes than could be packed into a suitcase, were offered passages to Australia, but preferred to wait for a steamer bound for England where they would be more likely to meet friends. Perhaps the extraordinary confidence in Singapore as a stronghold immune from the Japanese advance was derived from the placidity of the Government announcements on defence, one of which I remember, published in late January, was to the effect that every householder with a garden, no matter how small, was to be asked to grow vegetables for his own consumption and his neighbours'. Fertilizers were to be distributed by the Food Production Office. And this was when the Japanese were less than fifty miles distant.

It may have been that the Government was as ill-informed about the military position in Malaya as was the public, but this seems hardly likely. Be that as it may, from the very first day of the Japanese attack, the public of Malaya was kept in appalling ignorance of what was happening. News of the Japanese occupation of Kelantan for example, which took place on December 8th, was not publicized until December 22nd; and the press censorship was so severe that, even when Singapore was bombed for the first time, no true report appeared in the papers, which instead filled their columns with long accounts of the fighting in Libya and Russia. The climax came on January 29th when a BBC broadcast announced that Ipoh was suffering incessant bombardment from Japanese aircraft, although in fact the Japs were then within a few miles of Singapore and Ipoh had been in their hands over five weeks.

Meanwhile the Japanese were conducting propaganda and publicity on their own lines. Leaflets were dropped throughout the campaign, the text written in illiterate English, as well as Chinese, Malay and Tamil. "Evacuate your towns before we bomb them," they warned the Asiatics. "We are waging war only against the white devils." There were also leaflets in graphic form; some depicted a grossly fat European planter lolling in the shade with beer bottles stacked beside him, while his Tamil labourers toiled in the burning sun; while others showed a sun-tanned British soldier grilling a beef-steak while evacuated Indian soldiers sweated behind him at work.

The Japanese army had its own special leaflets. One ran as follows:

To the British Army

The conduct, which you the British soldiers behaved badly to the Japanese is never forgiven by both the God and the humankind. That is, you imprisoned the Japanese and put them into the leper-house, into the oil-tanks and moreover slaughtered the Japanese non-combatants.

Impress on your mind that you expect to be revenged fifty one hundred times as many as you behaved one.

The Nippon Army

What, I wondered, must the Malay villagers have thought? For months they had watched the convoys of lorries, artillery and Bren-gun carriers rumbling northwards. They had been amazed

17

at the strength of our forces; they had believed implicitly in the Government's declarations of their country's invulnerability. Then they were told that the Japanese had tried to land at Kelantan but had been attacked by British aircraft and had retreated, leaving behind only a few survivors. For a while there was no more news; then to their astonishment the roads filled with car-loads of European women and children, wealthy Chinese and Indians, all hurrying south, to be followed a few days later by the European civil servants, planters and miners. Rumours spread but still there was no news. Later came the mauled and battered remains of the defending forces that had passed northwards so confidently only a few weeks before. The Malays did all in their power to help the retreat, but how could they reconcile the optimistic news declarations with what they saw for themselves?

Towards the end of January the tension in Singapore was increasing as fast as the flow of evacuees from the mainland. The aerodrome at Seletar had become impossible to operate from; it was pitted with craters, most of the buildings were badly damaged, and Catalinas had been dispersed around the outlying islands.

As the situation worsened the question of evacuation was uppermost in my mind. Some of the wives left by sea about the middle of the month, others were flown out on January 21st, and soon there was only a handful of families left. I was glad I could stay with Pat. If the island was invaded, at least I should be with her. The Japanese, I had heard, had their own methods of dealing with Eurasian girls who had married Europeans.

I was attached during those last days to a motor transport pool helping evacuation from the mainland. Every day we drove across the Causeway some fifty miles into Johore, picking up evacuees and bringing them back to the island.

On January 28th I drove to Kluang, sixty miles upcountry on the railway line, and found there the usual gathering of refugee women and children. I picked up a dozen of them—all the lorry would hold—and started back in the dark. We had almost reached Johore when there was a scream from one of the women. I braked hard. There was a shout from the back.

"Don't stop we're being fired at!"

From the scrub came a hail of rifle and machine-gun fire.

I shot away as a grenade exploded at the side of the road. We reached the Causeway safely and I reported what had happened.

"I'm not surprised," grunted the officer I told. "You must have driven straight through the enemy lines—twice."

The next day Pat was evacuated.

When I reported late in the morning to the Signals Room at Seletar I found there only Flight Lieutenant Catt and four airmen.

"Has your wife packed?" the Flight Lieutenant asked tersely.

"I think so, sir. Why?"

"Then get her down to the docks; there's a ship sailing at 1.30. Look lively, man, you'll have to jump to it."

I looked at my watch. It was 12.40.

Dashing out of the Signals Room, I tumbled into our battered 1931 Morris and drove frantically to Cairnhill Road. As I skidded to a stop outside the bungalow it was already close on one o'clock.

"Pat," I yelled. "Pat, where are you?"

She came out of the kitchen, a pile of freshly ironed baby clothes slung over her arm. "What's the flap?"

"You're leaving by ship; she sails in half an hour."

"Oh, Charles, I can't. I'm not packed."

"There's no time for packing. Here, take this." I pushed a few things into a canvas grip, and hurried her towards the car. By the front gate she stopped.

"Charles, are you coming too?"

"We'll see when we get there."

"I shan't go."

For a moment we stared at each other beside the waiting car, then I looked up and behind me. A formation of Jap bombers, at less than 3000 feet, was heading straight towards us.

"Don't stand here arguing; we'll be blown to bits." I bundled her into the car, and we shot off towards the docks, at right angles to the approaching planes.

The dock was almost deserted as at exactly 1.30 in the middle of an air raid we tore across the bomb-cratered flats; deserted except for the *Wakefield*, and she was starting to pull up her gangway. Pat was rushed aboard, the last person but one to join the last ship that got away from Singapore. A second before she vanished between decks she turned, looked back at me and tried to smile.

"See you in Blighty, Pat," I cried. But even as my voice echoed back from the towering hull it came to me that Blighty, to the love Eurasian girl I had married less than a year ago, was as alien as another world. From now on each of us was quite alone; and it seemed to me that the chances of either Pat or I living through the next few days were pretty slim; and even if by some miracle we managed to stay alive, how could we hope ever to see each other again?

After the *Wakefield* had disappeared I walked numbly back towards the Morris. Along the waterfront, quays and warehouses were burning fiercely, and a pall of smoke, darkening the sky, drifted away towards the centre of Singapore. I climbed into the car and drove to our bungalow in Cairnhill Road. There I smashed everything that might possibly be of use to the Japanese, then changed into clean clothes—putting on a faded khaki shirt still warm from Pat's ironing-board—and, a little after three o'clock, drove back to Seletar. I found the aerodrome nearly deserted.

The next few days had about them an air of nightmare unreality. More and more troops, civilians and refugees poured into the island making for the supposed safety of Singapore. The roads were packed; food and water were had to come by; there was confusion but no panic. A pall of inevitability and acquiescence settled on the overcrowded island.

I was quite unable to trace 205 squadron, which, I was later told, had left for Java. I eventually joined up with a mixed party of troops and civilians working on the Bukit Timah Road, near Woodlands. They were building a roadblock. I walked across to a powerful thickset man clad in white shorts and a faded blue silk shirt. He was squatting on his haunches, hungrily munching a sandwich.

"What goes on?" I asked him.

He told me, in a lazy Australian drawl, that they were trying to block off the Bukit Timah Road; an idea which seemed to him "damned silly". He was, I thought, the sort of man to whom a lot of things would seem "damn silly"—a rugged, powerfully built fellow, a little over forty, with thinning ginger hair. His eyes were cold and intolerant, and his smile had little merriment in it. A tough customer. But tough or not, he believed in fair shares, and offered me half his food, not as if he were doing me a favour, but automatically as though any other procedure simply did not occur to him. In the months that followed I was to notice this trait again and again. No matter what the circumstances, it was, with Donaldson, always a case of share and share alike.

Conversation, at that first meeting, was not exactly easy. I told him briefly how I had rushed Pat aboard the *Wakefield*. He seemed interested.

"You married?" I asked him.

"Uh, uh," he grunted. And that was all I could get out of him—though I discovered later that he was in fact married, only he wasn't very popular with his wife, or (I forget which way round it was) his wife wasn't very popular with him.

That night, after posting sentries, we slept in scattered groups among the rubber trees of a small plantation. Stretched out with only the short grass beneath me—no pillow, no sheets, no mosquito net above me; no Pat beside me—I fell into a light, troubled sleep. The last I remember, as the kaleidoscope of the day's events whirled around my mind, reappearing and alternating with forebodings of the future, was Pat's attempted smile, and I heard through the pattern of my dreams the words "see you in Blighty" echoing and re-echoing, swelling ever louder in a harsh discordant crescendo.

Next day the roadblocking party to which I had attached myself worked on, adding bit by bit to the pile of stone and rubble which some of us optimistically thought would stop the Jap advance. But soon enthusiasm flagged, and we passed the time keeping in touch with neighbouring roadblock parties, obtaining and storing ammunition and cleaning our weapons. Then came the shelling of Singapore by artillery fire from across the Causeway. It was accurate fire, and made traffic almost impossible along the Bukit Timah Road. This, I realized, was the beginning of the last act, played to the accompaniment of almost continuous air raids. It was only a matter of time before the Japanese landed; and none of us were surprised when, early one morning, we heard through our bush telegraph that they had crossed the strait away to the west.

We decided to stay where we were—not that we had much option about it, for the shelling was maintained so consistently that by far the safest place was in the shelter we had built. I tried to persuade Donaldson that our only hope was to escape across the strait and take to the jungle in Malaya. But he was dead against it, and, once his mind was made up, Don had no time for a point of view opposed to his own.

"For Christ's sake don't be bloody silly," he snapped. "The Japs are coming over the strait in their thousands. What chance would we have getting through them? And how do we get across the water? I'm not a bleeding fish."

It was useless to argue with him.

The next night, while we sat hunched up under the trees discussing, not too optimistically, our chances of survival, a young Argyle private suddenly held up his hand.

"Listen a minute, chaps!"

We listened.

"Christ!" said Don. "It's quiet. What's happened?"

None of us moved. The gunfire had stopped. There was no sound but the soft slithering of leaves in the undergrowth, a couple of dogs barking in the distance.

"One of two things," a soft Scots voice broke in. "Either the Japs are wiped out or we're packed in."

For a few minutes none of us spoke: each of us putting his own interpretation on the sudden silence. After some discussion it was decided to stay where we were overnight, then next morning to split up into parties of two, each pair to act independently, as they thought fit.

So it was that the next morning found Don and I walking slowly through the rubber trees, jumping for cover whenever we spotted any Malays—there seemed to be hundreds of them drifting aimlessly about—and avoiding the main roads which were crowded with transport.

"Hold it, Mac," he snapped suddenly.

Approaching down a side road at a smart pace was a company of some twenty Japanese soldiers, headed by an officer and a European in civilian clothes. Up came our guns. We held our breath as the party neared us. We were puzzled by the civilian. He was well dressed, with a soft Panama shielding his eyes from the sun, and he was talking authoritatively to the officer beside him. He seemed to be in charge. A slight rustle behind made us spin round sharply, but it was only two more of our roadblock party who had caught up with us.

"What the hell's that civvy doing?" I whispered to Don.

"Let's find out." He stepped into the road. It was very much a mistake. A spray of bullets tumbled us into the undergrowth. My finger was curled round the trigger of my Tommy gun and I squeezed hard. Three Japs fell writhing on the dusty road.

"Chuck it, you idiot," yelled Don. "We haven't got a chance." He dropped his gun, raised his hands and stepped into the roadway. He was, of course, quite right. We hadn't got a chance.

Reluctantly I threw my gun into the bushes, got to my feet, lifted my hands and followed him. Behind me came the other two.

The Japs broke ranks and surrounded us. One of them kicked me hard between the buttocks, sending me sprawling to the ground. I tried to get up, and another kick sent me flat on my face. There seemed no point in inviting a third, so I stayed where I was. Don, who had spoken to the European, turned to me.

"This bastard says there's no point in fighting. We've surrendered."

I look across at the sleek, well-dressed European.

"And what the hell are you doing?" I asked him.

He ignored me and spoke to the officer, telling him in Malay—a language which he imagined none of us would understand—that we should only be a nuisance and ought to be shot on the spot.

Angrily I interrupted him.

"You bastard! Whose side are you on?" Again I was kicked flat and jabbed with a rifle butt. There was more talk, now in Japanese, while the soldiers kept us covered. Then the officer barked an order; the lot of us were herded together and the Japs, abandoning whatever mission they were on, turned back towards Singapore, leaving two of their number to bury the men I had shot.

"Sorry, Mac," whispered Don as we were marched down the narrow dusty road. "What a mess I've made of it."

"OK, Don." I rubbed the bony end of my spine tenderly. "We're lucky to be still alive."

Our muttering was stopped by a jab each from a rifle butt.

We were prisoners. Prisoners of war. The fact did not immediately seep into our consciousness as the Japs marched us south towards the smoke-smudged town. It had all happened so quickly—the one sudden encounter, then we were walking down the concrete road as though on a route march with a bunch of surly NCOs prodding us along. But I had killed three Japs; the Tommy gun had fired almost without my knowing; my fingers had pressed the trigger and three lifeless bodies had sagged on to the road. I looked around me at the flat, oval, expressionless, slit-eyed faces. Jap faces; enemy faces; breathing like mine, sweating like mine in the wet, sticky heat. They looked emotionless, but what were they thinking? Were Jap troops buddies with one another like our own men; if so, what were they storing up for me? Torture? Or were they perhaps as devoid of sensitivity as their faces seemed to indicate? Their expressions gave nothing away.

More troops and lorries passed us on the way to Singapore. A column of tanks rumbled by—amateurish-looking affairs, the metal strung together with no indication of strength or craftsmanship. But their crews looked efficient enough, smart and well ordered, primed with victory. Beside the road were several Malays staring wide-eyed at our passing procession, and at Newton Circus we were watched by groups of Tamils and Indians and a small number of Chinese.

Raffles Place, in the heart of Singapore, seemed untouched by the bombardment, and the beautifully proportioned buildings glared white in the sun against a sky every now and then fogged over by smoke drifting northwards from the docks. A great crowd of Europeans was milling around; some of them were being packed together by guards; others were being marched away over Anderson Bridge (mostly women and children, I noticed), while other groups were waiting listlessly, numb with despair.

We were marched over to the Mercantile Bank, where a mixed

party of Asiatics and Europeans, consisting of both servicemen and civilians, were shifting restlessly about under the guard of five or six armed Indians. The Indian Army, it seemed, had transferred lock, stock and barrel to the Japs; I noted that most of the guards were Indians, and they were revelling in their new-found power. I saw a Chinese shop-owner being clubbed to death by the rifle butts of four massive Indians, all wearing the King's uniform. Some of our party were sobbing, others were almost hysterical with terror. A few Asiatic women clung tightly to young children, while a group of prosperous-looking civilians muttered together, hopefully planning to buy their way to freedom. Donaldson was standing several yards away from me, and as none of us were allowed to move, I could not get across to him.

Without food or water we stayed there for the rest of the long, weary hours of daylight. We were there at dusk, and we were still there at midnight, by which time most of us had dropped to the pavement, huddled together for warmth. I dozed off, stupid and fuddled with fatigue. Early in the morning it began to rain. I awoke, and then fell asleep again, my shirt soaked, the water dripping from my hair.

The sun had just risen when I was kicked into consciousness by a hefty Sikh. I was about to kick him back when I remembered. And remembering was a nightmare. I spotted Donaldson, and with a wary eye on the Sikh guard who was striding over the sleepers and kicking them into life, I crossed over to him.

"Know what's cooking?" I asked him.

"I guess we're going to be questioned about why we didn't surrender on the fifteenth. Ceasefire was ordered that night and you, you stupid bastard, had to open up yesterday and kill three Japs."

"How the hell was I to know there was a ceasefire? You didn't know either."

"Huh," he grunted, "you try and convince the bastards of that!" He looked at me curiously. "And say, Mac, what are you going to tell when they ask what your occupation is?"

"Why RAF, of course."

"Do you think they'll believe you? You're not in uniform."

"I'm wearing a service shirt."

"A lot of good that is. Have a dekko at it."

I did and realized just a little of the sort of trouble I was in for. The shirt was dirty, but there was nothing khaki about it. It had been khaki once, but now it was bleached white from the sun and from its many journeys to the dhoby. My shoes too were of a civilian pattern.

"Christ, Don, they'll think I'm a spy."

He pulled is ear lobe thoughtfully. "Too bloody true, cobber."

I sat down and tried to think it out. But I was tired and hungry and couldn't reason properly.

About 2.30 that afternoon, still without food or water, some thirty of us, including civilians, were assembled and marched out of Raffles Square down towards the docks. Don found himself with some half a dozen other Australians and I joined up with them.

Abandoned cars cluttered up the roadside, and the pavements were littered with merchandise. Jap soldiers with fixed bayonets were half-running in and out of shops and offices, searching everywhere. Tamil labourers, under guard, were sweating in gangs of fifteen to twenty, working harder than I'd ever seen them work before. Here and there bodies lay about, the faces distorted and the blood hard and brown in pools beside them.

As we passed the railway station on the Keppel Harbour Road, I noticed two tins of food lying in the gutter. I stooped quickly and picked them up; one I shoved into a pocket in my shorts and the other I hid under my shirt. One of the Jap guards spotted me. He stopped the party, pulled me out of the line and shouted at me, gesticulating angrily. I gave him the tin out of my pocket, and he kicked me back into the ranks. A little further on I had another find—a service jackknife. I trod on it, knelt down and started fiddling with my shoelace. By the time the guard came up the knife had joined the tin under my shirt. We started off again, the Jap gibbering at me like a provoked monkey and prodding me with his bayonet.

West of the docks, we left the coast road and struck inland. Just before dark, about 5 pm, we came to a clearing in what was once a rubber plantation, not far from the sea. Here were a dozen or so half-finished atap huts, rickety on their supports; they were supported by deep coils of barbed wire. It was a small camp only about a hundred and fifty yards square. Beside the entrance gate was a dead Chinese hanging from a tree, his neck stretched and leathery, his swollen tongue black and covered with flies. At the foot of the tree sprawled two other bodies, grotesque and undignified in death.

Two at a time we were searched by a guard who gripped his bayonet, and was obviously anxious to use it. I lost the knife to him, but got away with the tin, which I had pushed under my left armpit.

Inside the camp several hundred British and Australian troops were mixed indiscriminately with a crowd of Asiatics. Excreta was everywhere underfoot and the smell was nauseating. The cage stank with a vile sweaty putrescence. Everyone was crouching apathetically either in the huts or near the wire, doing absolutely nothing. Don began to mutter with his bunch of Australians and I flopped down on my haunches, exhausted. After a little while I cautiously pulled the tin from under my shirt. It was condensed milk. Looking round, I saw a Tamil woman with a young child, her eyes fixed, without hope, on the small metal tin. I gave it to her, and she grabbed it eagerly.

Just before dark there was a stirring and shouting outside the cage, and a Jap officer, together with a European, stalked into the centre of the camp. Behind him trotted a soldier carrying a small wooden box. The officer halted, barked out an order and the soldier smartly smacked the box onto the ground. The officer stood on it and in pidgin English commanded that we stand to attention. I look around. Everyone was staring curiously at him but took not the slightest notice. The officer repeated his order several times, but there wasn't a stir. A young Tamil child started to cry. After a few minutes he gave it up, stepped down and strode off imperiously, followed by his small procession of NCOs and the European, who looked puzzled.

Night came and with it the blinding glare of hastily erected arc lamps, focused on the cage so that there was no spot unlit, except inside the few huts that retained some form of roofing. And with darkness came the mosquitoes.

I thought of Pat and her family in Sarawak. I wondered if the Japs had reached them yet. Perhaps they had been able to get away. But it seemed hardly likely.

As the night wore on the cage grew to resemble, more and more, a slough of human despair. The limp bodies of the captives moved restlessly in sleep or wakefulness, their faces etched in sharp relief under the glare of countless arc lamps. Unwashed Tamil bodies, unwashed British and Australian bodies, sweating, muttering troops, wailing children pitiful in their hunger, sick women crying softly, and one pathetic corporal suffering from shell shock and screaming. I stood up to stretch my legs. As I walked towards the wire, a burst of machine-gun fire flashed only a few feet above my head. I sat down quickly and cursed myself for the hundredth time for not having taken a chance and tried to reach Malaya on my own. After a little while it again started to rain; a fine incessant drizzle.

The drizzle developed in the early hours into a steady downpour, but towards dawn it eased off into continuous light rain. The earth between the huddled captives became a slimy quagmire; excreta and urine spread into the pools and soaked away, leaving in the heavy air a stench that retched the stomach. It was forty-eight hours since I had eaten, but I was at least no longer thirsty for I could turn my face to the sky, catch the rain on my tongue, and let it trickle slowly down my throat. That rain was nectar.

Soon I drifted into a sort of coma, the events of the last few days patterning in together like the pieces of coloured glass in a child's kaleidoscope; recollection and imagination separated, then linked together again; faded and then sharpened.

At dawn it was still drizzling steadily. The crowd stirred uneasily into wakefulness. Some of the Asiatics produced food—from God knows where—which they passed round among themselves. Three of the Australian soldiers had fixed up a sort of runnel off an atap hut which carried the rainwater into a tarpaulin and made there a small reservoir; so that we could at least help ourselves to a drink from the cigarette and fruit tins that most of us had managed to retain. We were a filthy looking lot, unshaven, dirty and sweaty. I passed a hand round my chin and scratched into the sticky, slimy beard.

Then I spotted Donaldson sitting alone and disconsolate a few yards away. I edged over to him and squatted down on my haunches, fishing out a packet of Double Ace cigarettes that I'd hidden in my shirt pocket; they were limp and stained brown from sweat and rain, but they were cigarettes.

"Smoke, Don?"

"Christ, where d'you get these?"

"I had 'em stuffed away in my shirt."

We looked round and noticed that several others had spotted the cigarettes. There was only one thing I could do.

"Anyone got a knife?"

"Sure." An Australian sergeant pulled one out of this handkerchief.

I cut each of the cigarettes in half and passed the pieces round. Don and I shared the last one.

The Tamil woman to whom I had given the condensed milk the night before came shuffling over and offered me a strange sort of leaf and a betel nut. I thanked her and she half-smiled and nodded before turning away.

"Try some?" I asked Don.

He looked at it dubiously. "Hell, I can't eat that stuff."

"More fool you," I grunted. I popped the nut into my mouth, and its bitter taste was as good as any food I had ever eaten.

I looked around at the scores of mixed prisoners in the camp, if camp it could be called, for in reality it was nothing but a collection of crumbling huts enclosed by massive coils of barbed wire, which had obviously been hurriedly thrown down. Almost touching the wire was dense and tangled vegetation, ten to twenty feet high. If only, I thought, we could surmount the wire, we would have a goodish change of losing ourselves in the undergrowth; but how to get over the wire?

Don was watching me closely.

"Hopeless on your own," he muttered.

"We could try to organize a party."

"You try, cobber. Half the fools here think the Japs'll be kicked out in a few weeks, so they're content to stick it out."

"Any idea where we are?"

"Well, they call the camp Pasir Panjang, but according to my reckoning we're nowhere near the place."

It was close to ten o'clock when we were lined up; the Asiatics were separated from the Europeans and marched out of camp; and those who remained were each given a stub of pencil and a printed form which we were told to fill in. I entered my name and address, my RAF number and my next of kin, stating Pat's address as "unknown". At any rate it seemed there was going to be some sort of system. Then we were told to stand up again and were counted off in twenties and marched out of camp, each party under two NCOs carrying Tommy guns. Don and I were together.

"Wonder where we're off to now," I muttered as we passed out of the wire enclosure.

"Maybe they're taking us to Changi. I've heard the troops are being sorted there." Don had a remarkable flair for picking up news.

"That cuts you out," I ribbed him. "You'll end up with the civvies. In jail."

"Civvy yourself," he grunted, glaring at my shirt.

But we were not destined that morning either for Changi or for jail. We were taken to the docks where a gang of Tamils were clearing filth and debris from the drains with spades and long wooden poles. It was there that we had our first taste of Jap corrective treatment. As soon as we arrived, the Tamils were told to stop work and to hand their implements to us. This they did, rather uncertainly and shyly at first; and we had no alternative, as we eyed the menacing Tommy guns, but to get to work. The Japs crossed over to the Tamil labourers and started talking to them. It soon became clear what had been said, for the Tamils began to boss us around.

"Work faster," one of them shouted to me in Tamil as he watched me sweating away.

I told him in his own language to go to hell. He picked up a spade and lashed out at my head; but I was quicker than he was, dodged out of the way and caught hold of the spade. I cursed him in his own language. He dropped his spade and scurried over to a Jap officer, crying out that I had sworn at him and tried to hit him.

The Jap officer walked slowly over, fingering his sword. This is it, I thought.

"Did you curse this man?" he asked, his face expressionless.

"Yes, I did. What right had he to start knocking me about?"

"Then you speak Tamil?"

I shrugged my shoulders, noncommittally.

"What is your name?"

I told him. He wrote something in his notebook and walked away. And that was that. But I wondered what would happen next, and just how soon it would be before I could expect a different sort of questioning. Interrogation it seemed to me was a certainty, for the Japs knew, first, that I was an RAF sergeant, a British subject; second, that I could speak Tamil with fluency; and, third, that I was not dressed as a serviceman, but as a civilian. All of which could easily make me in their eyes a spy.

Oddly enough, during that first day at the docks the Jap guards raised no objection when some of us, in between our bouts of drain-clearing, started to bargain for fruit with the crowd of watching Malays. We fairly stuffed ourselves with bananas and rambutans; and as at dusk we marched back to Pasir Panjang, we passed more Malays, from whom we obtained armfuls of bananas, and the guards seemed not the mind as we ate them on the way. Another example of Jap inconsistency came when we neared the camp. We were passing an odd groups of Tamils, Malays and Indians who watched wide-eyed as we slouched dejectedly along; most of them were quiet and impassive, but three or four Indians started cackling derisively, and one of them—a hefty six-footer—spat at us, some of his spittle landing on my face. I turned quickly out of line and booted him with all the force I could muster. The Jap guard ran up, turned the Indian round at the point of his bayonet and proceeded to kick hell out of him. Then he came back, smiled at me and we marched on.

"Queer lot, these Japs," I muttered to Don. "You don't know where you are with them. One minute they'll beat you up, and the next they grin at you."

"Shouldn't trust 'em too far, Mac, if I were you."

Back at camp we were each given half a Players cigarette-tin of rice and a sliver of salt fish; and then some of us made a big mistake. Having eaten their fill of fruit down at the docks, they had no stomach for rice and salt fish, so they threw it away. Over came the Jap guards and start to beat them up. Fortunately I was one of the last to get the ration, and I saw what was happening. I pretended to eat the food, but when the guards had left my part of the camp I tore a strip off the tail of my shirt, wrapped the rice and fish in it and stuffed the small bundle into my shorts pocket as a reserve. In the days that followed I was able to increase this small emergency ration by feeding off the fruit obtainable from the Malays down at the docks: this proved a godsend when, in the days to come, the Japs, as part of their corrective training, left us without any sort of food for five days.

That night—my third in captivity—when the arc lamps in the camp were switched on, and we were counted by the Japs, one sergeant was missing. How he had escaped none of us seemed to know, nor did we discuss it, for none of us could trust his neighbours as far as he would have wished. All of us had heard of the stool pigeon—the man pushed in to pick up information and pass it on to the guards. Any of us might have been a stool pigeon, especially as we were a mixed bag of both civilians and servicemen, Europeans and Asiatics. We didn't even know if we were in a permanent POW camp; though I personally assumed that we were in transit, for no serviceman had yet been properly interrogated, and furthermore in the days that followed, our numbers diminished steadily as each morning some of us were taken away—God alone knew where—and did not return.

The guards were unapproachable. There were three of them in charge of the working party I was in; two Japs, whom we dubbed Flatface and Fatarse, and a Korean, a grim, unyielding specimen known as Pigface. With the idea of getting information out of Flatface, I bartered my wristwatch with him for two bananas and ten Three-Star cigarettes. He knew he had he best of the bargain and he knew my motive for the exchange, but he told me nothing.

Then followed day after day, each bringing less hope than its predecessor, each making me more determined to get away whenever the slimmest chance offered itself; especially as I had heard that there was fighting upcountry. In the camp we grew to look like bearded scarecrows, and our daily ration—a half-tinful of rice and a minute sliver of fish—though it kept us alive, was very far from adequate. Several prisoners grew too weak and too ill to work.

But still each day we were marched, every one of us, over to the docks, where the Japs put us on a variety of jobs from clearing bomb rubble to burying Asiatic dead, of whom there were several thousand, mostly Chinese. One day we were instructed to reverse the procedure and open up the graves where less than a week before we had dumped the bodies on top of another like so many cattle carcasses. It seemed that for some reason only known to themselves, the Japs were trying to trace the body of a Chinese. It was a sickening experience. Burying the bodies had been bad enough; opening up the improvised graves was worse—much worse. We dug our spades into the earth dreading that jolt when the rusty metal would meet the solid mass of a skull or crunch through flesh into bone. Above us stood the watching guards, bellowing for us to work faster.

We dug for two days, and I began to wonder whether we were in fact searching for some specific body, or if our ordeal was part of the Jap corrective training. This latter idea was confirmed the next morning. As we were marching towards the docks, Flatface ordered us to halt and turn to the right so that we faced the verge of the scrub by the roadside.

There, only a few yards away, in a circle of dried blood, lay the body of a Chinese woman, naked except where the clothes had been pulled up round her head. She had been split cleanly from abdomen to breast with what must have been a single stroke, and the flesh had peeled back from exposure in the hot sun. White maggots were crawling over the bones, and, head downwards, the tiny skeleton of a baby was whitening inside the pelvis. With a sharp bamboo stake, the Japanese had murdered a pregnant woman. We were kept there twenty minutes, then came the order to turn left and we were marched off. Several of us were retching, and one man had fainted.

"Bloody bastards," muttered Don. "That's one form of bamboo treatment. God forbid we ever see the other."

But we did, a few days later, when a live human body was splayed out over an area of young bamboo shoots, arms and legs lashed firmly to stakes driven fast into the ground. In the tropical heat bamboo grows quickly—several inches a day—and the shoots are strong enough to be neither stopped nor diverted by the live flesh of a human body.

It seemed that the witnessing of such atrocities was almost to become part of our daily routine; for a few days later our party was marched out of camp along the main road to Newton Circus. There we were halted and joined by several other contingents from Pasir Panjang. We were turned to face a small group of Jap officers and NCOs. We thought we were going to be harangued about discipline, or lectured on the invincibility of Japan, or even told we were to be transported to new camps—until we noticed, a few yards from the Japs, three Australian officers under armed guard. There was no lecture. The Australians were brought forward, and we wondered what was happening when a Jap officer produced a packet of Craven

A cigarettes and in turn offered them one each. Surprised, they accepted, looking at each other speculatively. The Jap officer smiled broadly, showing a double row of large even teeth like a toothpaste advertisement; he lit the cigarettes, bowed, stepped back and then straightened up and barked out an order. A Jap NCO came forward. Quickly he plunged his bayonet into the Australians' stomachs. As they sagged to the ground, another Jap stepped smartly up, raised his sword high three times, and three times smacked it down on the Australians' necks, severing the head from the body.

Three of our party fainted, but were pulled upright by their companions. We were left standing there for several minutes, presumably so that we could comprehend the full impact of Jap omnipotence. Then another order was barked out, shattering the numbed silence. One of the Japs tied a length of cord round each of the heads and hauled it up onto the overhead tramway cable suspended above the road. The three heads hung there, blood dripping from the necks and seeping through the eyes, nostrils, ears and mouths. On the road three Craven A cigarettes swelled and disintegrated, each a pappy fibrous reminder in its pool of blood. The Japs were in no hurry to let us go. They kept us standing for another thirty minutes, but as last we were marched away, back to Pasir Panjang.

Strangely enough, I don't think the commandant of the camp was a willing part to these atrocities. He was a large fat man whose uniform stretched inadequately over his curves, shining in the places where it was constantly rubbed, and who wore his peaked cap perched perilously on top of his round, despondent face. He was not present at the Newton Circus murder and indeed we rarely saw him except when some slight favour was being shown to us, like the introduction of the daily barrel of drinking water. Unfortunately he was not in charge of us for very long.

A day or two before he was replaced, I suggested to Donaldson that we might ask permission for a sea bathe on our way to the docks. Don agreed there could be no harm in trying, so I approached Fatarse and questioned him in Malay. He said he would consult the commandant. Surprisingly enough permission was granted, and the twenty of us were allowed next morning to splash and swim in the sea for ten or fifteen minutes before continuing down to the docks for the inevitable clearing of bomb debris. We were exultant. We had at once the physical exhilaration of cleansing ourselves from layered sweat and grime and the mental stimulation of knowing that opportunism sometimes worked. That same evening the commandant addressed the camp. He told us that he was leaving; that he regretted the conditions we were living in, though the most he could do was to prepare a few suggestions for the attention of his successor. That evening six Army privates and one NCO, escaped from a working party. How they got away nobody seemed to know; except that the sea bathing had something to do with it. For those of us left behind it was an unhappily timed affair. For the new camp commandant arrived early the next day.

That morning we were assembled inside the barbed wire and our numbers were counted. The commandant stalked out in front of us; he was a skinny, surly looking little runt, his chin jutting forward and his eyes focused, not ahead of him, but on the sky. He was followed by a retinue of stooges, one of whom produced the inevitable soapbox for the commandant to stand on. He stepped on it and started haranguing us in pidgin English. His name, he said, was Colonel Nickar—but his rank badges I noted, were those of a captain. His speech was a short one. When it was over he stepped down and strutted off, his following of sycophants keeping step with him, including the soldier with the soapbox. The procession was pure comic opera.

But Colonel (Captain) Nickar was no comedian.

It was 9 am when he first introduced himself to us as we stood dutifully to attention. At 4 pm we were still standing, those of us who had collapsed being clubbed to their feet until they were supported by their friends.

Out stalked the commandant again and, as before, mounted his ceremonial soapbox. He started by explaining to us at great length how very good, kind and considerate were the Japanese and how ungrateful were we, the prisoners. We were the swine, he said. The Japanese were all "avenging angels". He stopped, suddenly and unexpectedly, and snapped his fingers. A dozen guards came forward and sorted out what seemed to be the tallest men in our company. They were mostly Australian. The guards passed me by, not noticing that I had slipped my shoes off and slightly bent my knees. Twelve prisoners were selected and marched out to between us and the commandant. Then he resumed his tirade.

"Last yesterday, British soldiers you asked sea bathing. I say 'Yes, OK, OK. You clean and then work!' Last yesterday seven soldiers ran away—very bad, very bad. We do not know where they go, very bad, very bad, most disgracious. However, must teach lesson, yes. Imperial Japanese Army masters of the world, liberators of all Asia. Must teach lesson!"

He banged his sword on the box.

The hands of the twelve prisoners were lashed behind their backs.

Twelve Japanese soldiers strode briskly forward and bayoneted them in throat and stomach. It was slickly done; within a minute they were dead.

A growl went up from the ranks. There was an involuntary surge forward, stopped short by a bursting of machine-gun fire. An Australian lieutenant whose quiet reserve we had always respected— he was the only officer among us—stepped forward, turned to us and shouted "Hold it, chaps, we can't do anything yet." He approached the commandant and we heard him tell in English that the Japanese soldiers had violated the rules of war. The commandant laughed and grunted something to one of his stooges, who cracked the Australian across his shoulders with a rifle butt. Three other Japanese seized him by the arms and started to drag him away. As he was carried off fighting desperately, he yelled out to us "OK, fellows, mark these bastards for future reference."

That was the last we saw of him.

Later we buried the twelve dead.

In the days that followed we became weaker and weaker, thinner and thinner, dirtier and dirtier, until we came to look like animals kept in some degrading cage. There was—needless to say—no more sea bathing. I cursed myself for having asked for the privilege in the first place; but Don pointed out that I had taken no part in the escape of the seven prisoners and that I need therefore accept no responsibility for the sequel. He was of course quite right. But the niggle was there. It still is.

A few days later the Japanese started sorting us out individually, and I knew that very soon they would get around to me. The first to be beaten up was a civilian whom we knew as Mr Pearson. One morning he was taken out of camp. Several hours later he returned, bruised, bloody and staggering. We crowded round and cleaned him up as well as we could with strips torn from our shirts. He had been tortured, we gathered, because a coolie had told the Japanese that he (Pearson) had robbed him of his wages. "Now," muttered Pearson, "we know that the new order's going to mean."

Day after day, civilians were taken out for interrogation. Some came back, some did not. Once a party of some fifteen Australians was marched off. They too never returned. Our numbers were getting smaller, and we grew resigned to doing nothing except exist from day to day and wonder whose turn it would be next. Our guards made no secret of the fact that most of us were "special" prisoners booked for "special" treatment. "You'll die in Singapore," they taunted us. And it seemed that they were very likely right.

Chapter Two

Inevitable there came the day when it was my turn—six weeks after being taken prisoner.

It was a bright morning and there was all the promise of a hot day. We were lined up as usual in our working parties, and counted by the guards. An orderly approached with a paper list in his hand.

"Sergeant Mar-orl-mac!" he shouted.

"Yes."

"Come with me."

I looked back at Donaldson, shrugged my shoulders, and tried to grin.

"Watch your step, Mac," he whispered as I stepped out of the ranks.

I turned to the orderly who stood staring at me.

"OK. Here I am,"

He stared even more intently, then he stepped forward and slapped my face. I couldn't dodge. He was too quick.

"Don't you know what you do when you face a Japanese soldier?" he barked.

I kept my temper and bowed, assuming that that was what he

wanted. It was.

"Wait here."

He left me and went round the other working parties, returning with four other prisoners, all civilians. A truck drew up and we were told to get in. We were driven some miles to a YMCA building on the shorefront near Collier's Quay, where we were handed over to a group of Japanese civilians. We were pushed into a room together and told not to talk. The truck moved off.

After a while I was called into another room where sat two Japanese civilians, an officer and a man who looked like a Eurasian. I glanced at them and they stared hard back at me.

The officer spoke first.

"You say you are Sergeant Mac-orl-mac?"

"Yes."

"What regiment?"

"No regiment. I'm in the Royal Air Force."

"Royal Air Force?" He glanced at the form in front of him. It was the one I had filled in soon after I was captured.

The Eurasian chipped in.

"You mean the Straits Settlement Volunteer Air Force?"

"No. The Royal Air Force."

"Where were you stationed?" This from the Jap officer.

"Seletar."

"What squadron?"

"Headquarters. No squadron."

"Do you fly?"

"No."

"On your form you state your address as Seletar."

"Yes."

"You are married?"

"Yes."

"Where is your wife?"

"I don't know."

"When did she leave?"

I wondered what he was getting at. The Eurasian interposed quickly.

"You were married in Singapore, weren't you?" I saw no reason to deny this or even hesitate.

"Yes."

"Your wife's name was Patricia Were?"

I paused. They seemed to know a good deal about me.

"Yes."

The other Japanese civilian jumped up.

"Why were you at Bukit Timah?"

"I was trying to join the rest of our chaps."

"Why didn't you leave Singapore with the other Royal Air Force personnel?"

"I stayed behind to help evacuate families."

They changed their direction of attack.

"Where did you live in Singapore?"

"Cairnhill Road."

"What number?"

"Eighteen, I think." It was Pat's mother's house. Were they after Pat's family? Surely not.

"You think?"

"Yes. We were there only a short wile."

"Who was your squadron commander?"

This was a trap that I was ready for.

"I was not on a squadron. I told you. I was at headquarters."

"Ah, yes. Where did you learn to speak Malay?"

"Malaya."

"How long have you been in Malaya?"

"Two years." I lied deliberately, to see whether they'd catch me.

"In two years you learned to speak Malay and Tamil and you got married?"

"Yes."

They went off on another tack.

"Sergeant, when did you last fly with the RAF?"

"I am not a flier now. I told you I was at headquarters."

"What is you job? What do you do in the RAF?"

There was no point in covering the truth. Besides, the "Sparks" badge was still on my shirt-sleeve.

"Radio."

"Ah, radio. Yes, indeed. But why did you not surrender when the others did?"

"I did not know about the surrender."

"So? You, a radio man, did not know about the surrender?" A Jap soldier moved up beside me.

"No. I didn't have a radio set."

"Liar!"

The civilian jumped up and slapped me hard across the face.

"I didn't have a radio set," I repeated.

He turned to the shelf behind him, piled high with junk. Like a performing conjurer, he seized a field telephone box, Army type, and banged it down on the table.

"This was yours."

It was a statement of fact, not a question. My mouth was smarting from the slap, but I had to smile.

"No. That is not mine."

"This is your radio."

He glared at me as if, by denying the fact, I was merely protracting the issue. I laughed.

"No. That is not my radio. It is not a radio at all. It is a field telephone generator."

He stared back, then abruptly stopped the interrogation.

"OK, OK, Sergeant. Go outside."

I waited outside in the hot sun for a long time, but the men with whom I had travelled to the YMCA hut that morning never came back.

"Where are my friends?" I asked the guard as I climbed into the back of the vehicle. He shrugged his shoulders and pushed me down onto the boards. We drove off in silence.

Back at the camp, darkness had fallen and I realized the interrogation had lasted a whole day. Donaldson made a beeline for me and, without saying anything, passed me some salt fish and a half-tin of water. He sat on his haunches, studying me with a quizzical look until I had finished eating. I told him what had happened.

"Did they do anything to you?" he asked.

"Only a swipe across the mouth," I said. I felt my face and hoped that the Jap had hurt his own hand half as much as he had hurt me. "It seemed just a formal check-up."

I asked him how he'd got on.

"Oh, usual mucking about. There's a rumour we're all going to Siam on some railway job; and there's another rumour that British troops have landed at Penang."

"Believe it?'

"Not bloody likely," he grinned.

He stretched himself out, his hands behind his head, looking up at the night sky, black and indefinite above the glare of countless arc lights. I looked around. Outside the wire Jap sentries were padding up and down, one of them doing something to the electric cables that lay on the wet earth, distributing power to the arc lights from the generator shed by the entrance to the camp. Beyond, the heavy leaves of the undergrowth were slithering softly in the light breeze; beyond the jungle, the sea. The sea. And on the sea Pat in the *Wakefield*. Pat with our baby. A girl. It had to be a girl. We had both wanted a girl. She would be sleeping, unconscious and unaware; no Japs, no war, no anything except the food she cried for (how many times a day had the book said?) and dreaming of Pat and of our daughter I had never seen, I fell into a deep untroubled sleep.

The next day was hell.

Once again my name was called, and once again I was taken to the YMCA building, but this time I was on my own and the procedure was very different from that of the day before. I wasn't just marched into the interrogation room; I was kicked through the doorway and prodded in the ribs by a rifle butt. "This is it," I thought.

At the table was a Japanese officer with a large flat head and a heavy, moon-like face—a face I shall never forget, expressionless and quite devoid of mercy. I stood in front of him waiting. He stood up, snapping his fingers. He was, I noticed, short and very broad, and from a belt around his waist hung a ceremonial sword, its handle beautifully worked in silver and semi-precious jewels. He stared at me hard. Then I was marched out again.

The guard grinned and cracked me across the back of the neck with his rifle butt. I gaped at him stupidly. Then he marched me in again. Again I faced the officer, swaying slightly on my feet, waiting. He spoke in English with a soft, purring, slightly American accent.

"When will you learn respect?" he whispered so quietly I could hardly hear him. He snapped his fingers again. Again I was marched out.

Outside the door, the guard grabbed me by the neck and forced my head between my knees. He did it again and again and again. Up and down, up and down, like a jack-in-the-box. The blood swam in my ears. On and on it went for what seemed like hours, but was probably no more than three-quarters of a minute. Then he kicked me to the floor, and again and again dug his rifle butt into my ribs. At last he jerked me to my feet and once more marched me into the room. The officer looked up. I knew what he wanted and bowed. The room slowly revolved around, then steadied. On the table were articles from my house at Cairnhill Road, including a Zenith radio set.

"Your name is Sergeant McCormac?"

I decided that politeness would pay dividends.

"Yes, sir."

"Royal Air Force?"

"Yes, sir."

"What squadron?"

"No squadron, sir. Headquarters."

He paused and looked at me hard. From the sheaf of papers by his side he produced a newspaper cutting, which I quickly recognized. It was from the *Straits Times* and showed Pat and myself dancing at a club in Singapore. On my uniform the air-gunner's brevet showed quite clearly.

"Do they have air-gunners at your headquarters?"

I began to realize what I was up against. "Sometimes, sir. Especially if they've been taken off flying."

"When did you last fly and with what squadron?"

"I last flew about a year ago. My squadron left some time ago."

"Where to?"

"I don't know."

He nodded at the guard, who slapped me across the mouth. Then he changed his tactics.

"Your wife is Eurasian."

I did not answer, and the guard clouted me across the back of my neck.

"Your wife is Eurasian. We know that from the picture. Where are her parents?"

The questioning had shifted now to Pat and Pat's parents; but to what purpose? I dared not contemplate what the Japs would have done to Pat as a punishment for marrying a European, had she stayed in Singapore. But she was at sea. Would they try to find her people and revenge themselves on them?

"I don't know, sir."

"You don't know very much, do you?"

I did not answer.

"Why did you open fire and kill three Japanese soldiers after the surrender?"

So we were back to that.

"I didn't know we had surrendered."

"You were engaged on flying Catalina aircraft from Manila to Singapore, yes?"

The officer was opening up now. I did not reply. He waited and then went on.

"Sergeant, 205 Squadron had Catalinas and they operated from Singapore. That we know. Where is their base now?"

"I don't know, sir."

"Liar!"

He nodded to the guard. I tried to dodge the blow but couldn't. It was a mistake to have tried, for the rifle butt caught me on the forehead just above the eye. A trickle of blood oozed down and I could feel the flesh thickening over the lid. Somehow I had to convince him he would gain nothing by having me beaten up.

"Listen," I said. "If you want to punish me for shooting after the surrender, go on and get it over with. But I don't know what else you want. I can tell you nothing. Nothing. I am only a sergeant."

The officer pushed the papers away from him, then turned away and looked out of the window. He did not meet my eyes, but said, smoothly and caressingly: "All right, Sergeant." He paused, still gazing through the window into the far distance, then: "Sergeant, would you like to meet your wife?"

I was stunned, and stared at him open-mouthed. Had they got Pat? What could I believe of this man? I did not answer and he turned to watch me.

"We can arrange for you to see her."

"My wife is not here."

52

One of the guards gripped my arms from behind, while another again and again jabbed his rifle butt into my stomach. Foolishly, I lost my temper.

"You bastards!" I cried. "I can't answer your damned questions. I'm not supposed to answer them. I don't know anything, I tell you."

The soft purr went on as if the speaker had never heard me.

"When did your wife leave?"

I did not reply. One of the guards lifted his knee and jerked it deep into my stomach, bringing the saliva up through my teeth. Then, as I slumped forward, he back-handed me across my mouth.

"When did your wife leave?"

Did it matter if I told him? It was over six weeks since the *Wakefield* had sailed; she must have reached safety long ago.

"At the end of January."

"Where was she bound for?"

"I don't know."

Another kick.

"What boat did she leave on?"

"The *Wakefield*."

"How many left by that boat?"

"I don't know."

"Where are your wife's parents and relations?"

"I don't know."

My interrogator frowned. He ran his finger strokingly along the side of his nose. Then came the soft purr again.

"I must tell you that the *Wakefield* was sunk. There were few survivors. If your wife is among them I will take you to her, but you must answer my questions first."

If your wife is among them! If! Then, when he had told me before that Pat was alive, he must have been lying! Oh God, what was I to believe? "The *Wakefield* has been sunk ... few survivors." I felt sick. The room swam round me, and in the centre of it, I saw that the officer had risen and was walking round the long table towards me. He was unsheathing his sword. He stood directly in front of me. Whether or not he was moving the blade I do not know, it certainly seemed like it, but perhaps my eyes were out of focus. My arms were again pinned behind me. I was helpless. He jabbed the sword at my face. I turned away sharply but could not avoid it. It caught me under my right eye, laying open the flesh; and the blood gushed down into my mouth and all over my shirt. I struggled desperately and managed to kick one of the guards in the groin. It was a mistake. I was grabbed and kicked in the stomach, again and again. I wanted desperately to vomit, but couldn't. The sword was a second time circling in front of me. I tried to hunch my head between my shoulders, but the blade slithered sharply through the flesh below my lip. Another stream of blood. Blood trickling down my throat, and my mouth drooping loosely.

"Now will you answer me?"

"What do you want?"

He sighed and laid the sword on the table, then spoke rapidly to the two guards, who tightened their grip on my arms. He went back to his seat the other side of the table.

"We have received information that your wife and her family are dangerous to us."

"Why should my wife be dangerous? She is only a girl. She knows nothing of war." My voice was thick and husky through the blood.

"Her family is dangerous; are they in Borneo?"

"I don't know."

"Answer me."

"I don't know."

"You are a wireless engineer?"

"Yes."

"And your wife's father? What is he?"

He was, I knew, supervisor of telegraphs and wireless at Kuching in Sarawak. If I told them this, would any harm come of it? I could not think clearly and the room was dizzying around me. Better be on the safe side. I mumbled foolishly.

"I don't know what his occupation is." It was an idiotic answer.

"You are a liar."

A succession of back-handers lashed across my mouth. My gums were swelling up; my lips felt like puffed-up sausages. Then I blacked out.

When I came round again, the officer was still there, watching me.

"Now, will you answer me?"

I stared at him stupidly and tried to answer. But I had no strength to form the words. I heard a strange guttural grating from the back of my throat. My head was jerked forward from another blow on the back of the neck. Then came a merciful darkening whirlpool that was the room and the Japanese faces and a singing, echoing crescendo of noise as I dropped unconscious to the floor.

How long I lay there I shall never know; but when I came round I was alone. I moved, slowly, carefully, feeling my body, arm and legs, and turning my neck from side to side.

The pain was excruciating. After a little while I tried to sit up, and at once two Jap soldiers came in. They pulled me to my feet, pushed me down a few steps and out into the fresh air (it was still daylight) and left me propped up against the steps like a battered tailor's dummy. Then the officer came walking past me, fingering his sword. "I shall be seeing you again," he said. "Next time you will be more sensible."

Then the guards pushed me into the back of a captured British truck. As we drove off, I asked one of them (in sign language) for a rag to clean up my face which was caked with congealed blood. I was given, not first aid, but a vicious blow across the mouth, and again the blood came seeping through, thick and glutinous. My hands were bloody, my stubble of beard was bloody, my shirt and shorts were bloody, even my legs were bloody.

At Singapore railway station the truck halted and we had to walk. It was dark by now and raining. I could not stop shivering and vomiting blood and mucus, and thought I was probably in for a bout of malaria. I thought wildly of trying to make a break for it. But I was too weak, and felt that, if they caught me—as they were bound to—there would be another beating-up, and that I could not face. So I staggered with them the five miles back to camp. At last we reached the guard enclosure and there I was told to wait. I waited for something like two hours, shivering without shelter in the rain; then Pigface came out, opened the wire gate and kicked me inside the cage. Japanese boots have split toecaps made of very hard leather, and a kick really hurts. Just inside the wire a fresh contingent of Malays and Chinese lay huddled close together, most of them dozing or sleeping;

but over the other side I spotted the Europeans and half-staggered, half-crawled towards them.

I found Donaldson and prodded him into conscious. He blinked at me sleepily in the hard light of the arc lamps.

"Jesus, Mac, are you back? We'd given you up. By God, man, what a mess you're in."

He grabbed his drinking-tin and forced some rainwater between my lips, then tore a strip of cloth from my shirt, dipped it into the tin and gently, oh so very gently, started padding away the dried blood from my face and body. He was nurse, wife and mother all in one. I felt like a child as he did all he could to ease my pain. Halting I began to tell him what happened, but he put his finger to his lips and nodded warning towards a guard who was watching us. Carefully he laid my head down.

"Don," I said, "there's a hell of a lot you must know."

"OK, cobber. But let it wait until tomorrow."

"But Don, he said they'd sunk the *Wakefield*; he said there were only a few survivors."

"Had you told him Pat was on it?"

"Yes, I had to."

"Then pay no regard, he was trying to break you down. Forget it."

"My God. Don, if they've killed Pat ..."

But Donaldson had closed his eyes, and soon he was asleep.

Chapter Three

That night I was obsessed by nightmare fears, dozing fitfully whenever I managed to find a comfortable position, then awaking with a jerk as some new pain cramped my muscles. I resented Donaldson lying untroubled beside me, his mouth open, his snoring echoing loudly into the night. The *Wakefield*, the officer had said, had been sunk; there were few survivors. "Few survivors?" or "a few survivors"? Which had he said? One offered more hope than the other. "Would you like to see your wife?" he had asked. "We can arrange for you to see her." Was that the truth or a trap? I thought back over the questioning and recalled that he had paused before telling me the *Wakefield* had been sunk. Why had he paused? Was he thinking out how best he could use the news to get information from me? Or had he invented the whole story? I couldn't work it out.

Long before dawn I was awake, squatting on my haunches, my stomach sore as if it were lined with sandpaper, the sword-cuts round my right eye and mouth oozing yellow water where the flesh lay open. I was terrified of what the day might bring. Would I once again be singled out for "special interrogation"? How much more, I wondered, would I be able to stand.

On the other side of the camp the new contingent of Chinese and Malays were stirring uneasily into wakefulness as the sunlight spread over the coils of wire and cast long, welcome shadows over the huddled figures. What a scene of human misery it was. Poor bastards, I thought, poor bloody bastards. This was the darkest, cruellest part of war.

Donaldson stirred and blinked at me through sticky, half-closed eyes. He ran his hands through the ginger tangle of his hair.

"Christ, Mac, what a mess you're in!"

"They didn't provide me with a mirror. I'm sorry I couldn't tidy myself up for you."

"Easy up, cobber," he grunted. "I'm sorry."

I told him about the interrogation, about the beating-up, the news of the *Wakefield* and of the questions they'd asked me about Pat's family. He made little comment, offered little sympathy and gave me little advice. That was the sort of man he was. He believed in action rather than speech or thought. With death and bestiality all around us, I suppose he could see no point in discussing the chances of Pat still being alive. Perhaps I should not have expected him to. He had known me for only a few weeks, and Pat to him was nothing but a girl's name. While I went rambling on with "ifs" and "buts" and tried to draw him to argue out with me the pattern of the interrogation, he grew more and more silent. My nerves were on edge; now, more than at any time in my life, I needed help and sympathy.

"My God, Don!" I blurted out at last. "Tell me what you think, man. Was the *Wakefield* sunk? Was Pat one of the survivors? Say something, can't you?"

He looked at me helplessly.

"Sorry, chum. Honestly, I wouldn't know."

"But what do you think?"

"Well, if you must have it, I should say the chances of the *Wakefield* getting away are pretty thin. Stands to reason, doesn't it? But ..." he saw my face fill with despair, "... there's always a chance, cobber, so keep on hoping."

I rose unsteadily to my feet. My head pounded. I thought I was tough, but at that moment I was pretty near to tears. The guards were starting to line us up for the morning parade.

"Listen, Don, I don't know that I could stand another dose of torture. If they start carting me away this morning, I'll take a chance and run for it. At least I might get a quick death that way."

"Steady, Mac, what hope would you have."

"At any rate they wouldn't get a line on Pat's family."

Don looked at me curiously.

"You're not serious, are you?"

"Sure I am. Figure it out for yourself. What would you do in my place?"

"OK, Mac. Do what you have to do. But remember what'll happen to the rest of us."

I couldn't grasp his meaning.

"What?"

"Well, there's twenty of us in our working party. If you happened to get away, don't you realize they'd bayonet the rest of us, like they did my cobbers."

I hadn't thought of that. "Too bloody true," I said slowly.

Then the guards were pushing us into line. In between the huts parties were being lined up, counted off and marched out of the camp.

Here and there the guards pulled out a prisoner for the day's "special treatment". I watched their progress from one party to another with helpless and desperate terror. Pigface approached our contingent, reading deliberately through a printed list; he looked straight at me, grinned maliciously and passed us by.

"Thank God for that," I whispered.

The wounds on my face throbbed painfully as we were marched down to the docks, and the bruised flesh on my buttocks pulled painfully against the bone at the base of my spine. I loped forward from the hips trying to stop my muscles stretching.

Don was walking beside me. Both of us were thinking, with a new urgency, of the possibility of escape.

After a while, he said quietly, "Look, Mac. I've got an idea. Suppose the whole lot of our working party escaped—all twenty of us. The Japs would nobody left to take reprisals against."

I looked at the men marching alongside us; we were a tough, desperate-looking bunch. Could we manage it? And if we did, what were the chances of survival in the jungle?

"Where would we make for?" I whispered. "Malaya, perhaps. Then across to Sumatra."

"Why not Australia?" grinned Don.

"Two thousand miles. One of us might make it, perhaps; God alone knows how."

"I doubt if we'd get the rest of the bunch to try it," Don muttered. "But there's no harm in finding out. I'll sound them out when we get down to the docks.

During the day, choosing his time carefully when the guards weren't watching, Don edged his way from man to man. I sounded one or two out myself, keeping a wary eye on the guard who was watching my end of the working party. He was a swarthy fellow; fat, round-faced and in his early forties. He didn't look like a Japanese, and it came to me suddenly that he might well be a Portuguese Eurasian. I also had the feeling that I had seen him somewhere before. Anyhow, his behaviour was distinctly odd. Whenever the other guards approached he would turn to us and snarl and bellow. But when they turned their backs, he would whisper to us in a sympathetic, friendly manner and tell us to ease up while the others were not looking. Early that afternoon he slipped one of our men a cigarette and to another he gave a handful of rice. All the same I didn't trust him and waited until he was out of the way before enlisting support for our proposed escape. But oddly enough he didn't leave me very often; he kept on glancing at me, quizzically. I couldn't make him out.

As we were marching back to camp that evening, I told Don about him.

"Ruddy stool pigeon, I expect," he expect," he said. "We'd better watch our step there."

"What do the others think about escape?"

"They don't like the idea too much. Three or four were game to try anything; a few others were willing to join up if we had a decent plan; but the rest were dead against it."

We entered the cage at Pasir Panjang that night with more than usual weariness. I cannot remember having ever been so completely exhausted; my whole body was aching with bruises; the cuts on my face had stopped seeping but were now smarting painfully from the salt of my own sweat. The open wounds attracted a multitude of minute, irritating bacteria, especially when night fell and the damp stench of the camp offered a rewarding hunting ground for the flies and mosquitoes winging their way from the thick undergrowth and jungle around the barbed wire.

I was depressed at the lack of enthusiasm for a mass escape, but as Don pointed out, this was not perhaps surprising since we had had no definite plan to put forward. In the days that followed I expected, at any moment, to be pulled out of the party and taken for more interrogation; and this gave an added urgency to the countless schemes that formed and half-formed in my mind, only to be rejected in the final analysis as offering no real chance of success.

Then came the sort of opportunity I had been desperately hoping for.

Five days after my interrogation we were working as usual on the docks when the fat Eurasian came up to me.

"Don't stop working," he muttered. "Don't let the guards see you talking to me."

"OK." I went on piling up the stones, bricks and sludge.

He turned his back on the two Japanese, who were talking together further along the line.

"You don't remember me, do you?"

"Can't say I do. Should I?"

"I'm Rodriguez. I used to work up at the aerodrome."

So that was where I had seen him. I ought to have remembered.

"Of course, Rodriguez, I remember you now."

"Careful," he whispered, and strolled away as the two guards approached us.

But soon he came back and we went on talking. He had little news to tell me of what had happened at Seletar. I asked him if he knew what had happened to the *Wakefield*, and he said he thought she had been sunk.

"Were there any survivors?"

"I don't know. I haven't heard of any."

I looked away. My grief was not the sort that should be seen or shared.

"You're been tortured, haven't you?" he asked softly.

"Yes, and I'm expecting more."

"Why don't you try and get away?"

I looked at him curiously. How far, I wondered, could I trust this man? I decided to take a chance.

"I've thought of it, of course."

Rodriguez leaned closer to me. "Then be quick. I tell you, you won't live long at Pasir Panjang. Most of you here are held as being specially dangerous. One by one you'll die."

Now I was learning something. Now I knew it was escape or die. Rodriguez hesitated a minute, looked at the guards, who were well out of earshot, then whispered very quickly.

"I have a brother in Malaya. Up in the hills near Kuala Lipis. He's with the guerrillas. I could fix a boat for you to cross the strait. Perhaps you could join up with them."

"How much do you want for helping us? I have no money."

It was Rodriguez's turn to look away.

"I ask no payment. The Japanese raped my daughter."

Back in camp that evening, Don and I put our heads together. We thrashed out every possible way of escape. For one or two men several alternatives presented themselves; but we, to avoid reprisals, must get the whole working party away. It seemed a pretty hopeless task. But now we knew that we could not expect to be treated as ordinary prisoners, any desperate chance seemed to me worth seizing. And that evening we had further evidence of the urgency of our position. The guards were in good form. Amid roars of laughter they explained to us in detail and no fine point omitted, that they had been to watch a mass execution—the beheading of twelve Chinese and Malays suspected (only suspected) of being anti-Japanese. Doubling up with laughter and slapping each other hilariously on the back, they gestured and gyrated their hands in a downward spiral pantomiming the victims' heads as they rolled away from the executioners' swords. Those heads might soon be ours.

Our nerves had by now become taut and strained. In my own case, despair for the future alternated with the deepening conviction that Pat was dead. For us in Pasir Panjang the accepted standards of civilized life were remembered only distantly, as though belonging to another world. The old familiar routine of daily living had vanished; it had been replaced by a more primitive pattern of life—the animal instinct to survive. This new existence did not seem to us a dream. All that was past was the dream—sleeping in bed, shaving, baths, good food eaten with cutlery, newspapers, pyjamas, clean underclothes, beer, having a wife, the promise of becoming a father—all these were memories from a half-forgotten world; misty images from a fantasy long ago experienced. Now there was only one reality—survival; a survival that entailed sweat, hunger, filth and Japanese barbarity. We were animals. Given the chance of freedom, we would fight savagely and we would die miserably. Logic was reduced to very simple terms. Don and I recognized that logic. It was escape or die.

"Let's sound out our party again about escaping," I said. "Now

Rodriguez will help they may come in with us."

We went round the next day tackling each man individually, trying to convince him of the futility of simply waiting to be killed. The result was better; much better; but there were still six men who wouldn't at any price join in.

The solution came to me suddenly.

"Listen, Don. There's no roll call in the camp. To the Japs our working party consists simply of seventeen Europeans and three Asiatics. The Japs aren't interested in names. All they worry about is numbers. Six of our men won't join in; all we need do is go round the rest of the prisoners tonight, find six chaps willing to come in with us and swap them for the six who won't."

Don smiled slowly and then smacked his fist with other palm.

"You've got it, Mac," he said.

It was as simple as that. By the cold light of the arc lights, we crawled from one party of men to another and quickly found six who were keen to make the attempt. The actual method of the escape was left to Don and me to work out, though it was agreed that we would all stick together and, once we had got away from the camp, make for Rodriguez's boat and thence over to the mainland to join the guerrillas. None of the Asiatics could be trusted to join in so the escape was planned for the seventeen Europeans only.

The first step was to keep Rodriguez informed of our intentions. He was on duty the next day at the docks and I told him that the whole working party, including the six new men (whom he hadn't noticed until I pointed them out) had decided to attempt an escape. We knew what our fate would be if we were recaptured, but we were, I told him, determined to go through with it.

He did not look too happy.

"How do you propose to escape?" he asked, rather fearfully.

"That will come later. But we'll definitely need your boat. You won't let us down, will you?"

His mouth took a firmer line.

"No."

"OK then. I'll tell you when we're set."

He fidgeted uncomfortably.

"You can't do it during the day, while I am in charge of the party. I have a wife and six children to think of. You'll have to do it at night. Then suspicion won't fall on me."

"That's fair enough."

"Which night will it be?"

"Don't know yet. Probably tomorrow."

"All right. If you get away tomorrow night, come to my house at Paya Lebar and I'll take you to the boat. Do you know Paya Lebar?"

I said I did. It was a tiny village a couple of miles from Seletar airfield on the Serangoon Road, and about twelve miles from the compound at Pasir Panjang.

"How will I recognize your house?"

He gave me full details of how to find it.

That evening at Pasir Panjang, Don and I studied the gate into the camp. It was only a flimsy affair—a nine-foot bamboo bar entwined with barbed wire which was lifted up by the sentries whenever we entered or marched out. A few yards outside the compound, to the left of the gate, was an atap hut, used, we suspected, as a powerhouse or control hut; here, obviously, was the main switchgear for the arc lamps. Round the camp, which was of course patrolled by sentries, was the electric wiring that fed the arc lamps and was connected at intervals by junction boxes. Between us and that heavy flex lay the coils of barbed wire.

I stared at the electric flex and the junction boxes, and a very simple plan began to take shape in my mind.

I have abnormally long arms. If only I could stretch through the barbed wire, I might be able to pull the leads out of a junction box and so disconnect the circuit. The compound would be plunged into darkness; in the confusion the seventeen of us could charge the gate, and if we got through make a dash for it.

I explained my idea to Don. It was the sort of simple, uncomplicated scheme that at once appealed to him.

"That's it, Mac. You've got it. If only you can reach through to a junction box."

"Let's try," I said.

We waited until the guards were out of sight then crawled slowly towards the wire. Face downward, I pressed my arm carefully through the coils, twisting and turning it to avoid the barbs. My hand was still eighteen inches from the box. I couldn't do it.

Don was crouching beside me.

"There's only one thing for it, Mac," he whispered. "Ease your head through one of the coils. I'll push the wire up, then maybe you can make it."

"Don't touch it now," I muttered. "The noise of the wire grating will bring back the guards." I quickly gauged the distance, and reckoned that with my head through the first roll of coils I would just be able to grasp the box. We slid away on our bellies.

That night the plan was passed on, in whispers, from one to another of the seventeen. We were each of us to find any weapon we could lay our hands on—a stick would be better than nothing. The attempt would be made the next day at dusk, just after the arc lights were switched on. We would rush the gate, force up the bar then scatter singly for the jungle, and reassemble later at Rodriguez's house. If any one of us was wounded or left behind, there was to be no returning for him, no waiting, no help. He would be left. It was a grim prospect, and that night few of us slept.

One possibility especially terrified me. What if the officer decided to interrogate me again the next day? The prospect haunted me as I lay staring at the night sky. I though about the wiring system too, and decided to alter the plan slightly. For it occurred to me that if I disconnected the circuit just before the lights were switched on rather than just after, the sudden release of the power load when the Japs switched on would have no escape and might, if there were no adequate fuse precautions, blow the switch-box.

Next morning the parade took place as usual. We were counted and, by the grace of God, none of us were held back for interrogation. We marched, in the coolness of early morning, down to the docks. All of us were nervously excited. Two or three set up a tuneless whistling, partly, I suppose, to relieve their tension and partly out of pure bravado.

"Shut up, you idiots," hissed Don.

The guards looked around threateningly and, with shame-faced grins, the warblers stopped their whistling.

Down at the docks, through the long, hot morning and longer and hotter afternoon, we sweated at clearing rubble. Sweated from the sun's heat, but sweated even more from nervousness at the thought of what the evening would bring. Thank God that once we were back in camp we would not have long to wait.

We told Rodriguez.

"I'll be expecting you tonight then," he quavered. And the trepidation in his voice made us more nervous still.

Every ordeal must, I suppose, end some time, and when at long last we were paraded again for the march back to Pasir Panjang each of us had managed to find and conceal some sort of weapon. I had a thick club-shaped piece of ironwood. Don had a lump of lead and three to four feet of thin rope, which he knotted to the heavy metal, making a primitive bolo. It was a fearsome arsenal hidden that evening under our shirts and shorts, but the guards spotted nothing.

Back in camp we wasted no time; each man had his own part to play and knew exactly what to do. Alone or in couples, the seventeen of us, laughing and chattering, infiltrated towards the gate. This manoeuvring went on for over half an hour, by which time Don and I and two others had edged towards the barbed wire to where the nearest junction box was positioned. My heart was pounding deep inside me like the beat of a ship's engine. I wiped the sweat off my forehead.

It was getting dark now. In only a few minutes the Japanese sentry would be crossing over from the guard house to the atap hut where the switchgear and generator were.

I looked carefully around me, and saw some of our party eyeing me expectantly. Two guards passed on their routine patrol round the perimeter. It would be six and a half minutes before they completed the circuit. I took a deep breath.

"OK, Don," I muttered. "This is it."

Taking my time, I flattened out on the earth, then, lying at full stretch, started to slither carefully towards the coils of wire. Don was watching the disappearing guards; at strategic points four other lookouts were posted. They had their backs to us and were apparently disinterested; but each at the right moment gave a prearranged signal, and Don leant towards the wire.

"Coast is clear, Mac," he muttered.

He pressed backwards onto the first coil, and I heard his hissing intake of breath as he heaved against the taut wire. I slipped my left arm over a spiral of barbs, and eased my head through the first coil. My fingers, stretched out, were still a foot from the junction box. The barbs were digging into my left shoulder and blood trickled down my face as the sharp barbs tore through hair and skin.

"Not quite," I panted. "Press back as hard as you can."

Don grunted and I felt the wire tightening under the weight of his body. I squirmed forward with the wire, inch by inch, until I could stretch no further. My face was almost at right angles to my shoulders, twisted away from the lacerating spikes.

"Another two inches." The sweat was running down under my armpits. It tickled.

"Don, I can't see what I'm doing."

"Move your fingers left," he grunted.

I did—and touched the electric cables.

"Buck up, Mac, for Christ's sake!" panted Don. "The guards are coming back. They're only fifty yards off."

I gritted my teeth and jerked the cable sideways. The barbs bit deep into my shoulder and neck; but the strands, thank God, were loose in my hand.

"OK, Don."

I slithered back towards him, wincing as, for the last time, the barbs tore into my flesh. Some two or three yards inside the wire we half-rose and squatted on our haunches. The sentries ambled by, glanced at us curiously but seemed to notice nothing amiss and carried on round the perimeter.

The others were in scattered groups now on either side of the gate, silent, watching and waiting. Waiting for the Jap soldier to appear from the guard hut and cross to the powerhouse.

It can only have been a couple of minutes before we saw him strutting cockily across, but to each of us the minutes seemed like hours. We tried not to look at him, but I for one, each time I tried to look away, felt my eyes slide back to the short, bespectacled little man who would, in a matter of seconds, open for us the road to freedom.

He stared at us and seemed to sense that something odd was happening; then shrugging his shoulders he disappeared into the powerhouse. Almost as one man, in the gathering darkness, we started to edge towards the gate. We were none of us prepared for what happened next. We heard a generator start up, then a sudden, blinding flash lit up the huts, silhouetting its broken supports, its windows and its disintegrating walls. The sharp crack of an explosion echoed across the compound. The roof caved in and burst into flames.

For perhaps a couple of seconds we stood rooted to the spot, staring in disbelief. One man swore softly, another let out a ghastly cackle of laughter.

"Now!" shouted Don, and we tore towards the gate. Men shrieked in pain as the vicious coils of wire lacerated their hands, but we lifted the bamboo far from out of its socket and flung the gate up and over. At the same moment a handful of Japanese rushed out of the guard hut. For a second they wavered, then came the staccato crackle of Tommy guns, ending abruptly as we threw ourselves on them. I was lucky. I got Pigface. I saw him tearing towards me, his teeth bared, his bayonet swinging back; with all my strength I smashed the lump of wood down and onto his face. As he dropped, I lashed at him again. I heard the bone splintering and his skull felt oddly soft. I dropped my club, grabbed his bayonet and sprinted for the rubber trees. Behind me, the outline of struggling men stood out sharply against the glare of the burning hut. No going back we had said. I tore on. I passed Donaldson; he was struggling and jerking at what looked like a dead body.

"Come on, Don!" I yelled at him. Behind us machine guns were chattering angrily. I dared not stop. I was running now through tangled undergrowth, dodging quickly from one tree to another. Then I was in the open, and felt the sharp blades of lalang grass whipping against my legs. On and on I rushed, my lungs heaving like bellows, until at last I could run no further. I slowed down to a walk. But already someone was catching up with me. I could hear him crashing his way through the rubber plantation. I stopped in a little hollow, and crouched there, waiting. It was Don. He almost tumbled headlong over me, but at the last moment spotted me in the flickering light from the guard hut, now some quarter of a mile behind us.

"All right, Mac?" he panted.

"Uh, uh." I squatted there gasping for breath. "My wind's gone."

"Don't wait, for Christ's sake."

We went on, zigzagging whenever we were able, sometimes running, sometimes trotting, sometimes stumbling. Behind us the sounds of fighting grew fainter and finally died away. Both of us were breathing heavily and raspingly. But we were exultant.

"Why on earth were you hanging about outside the gate?" I panted, as we slowed down to a walk.

"Fatarse had my bolo."

"Good Lord, man! Why ever did you stop for that?"

"I dunno. The ball had stuck in his head and wouldn't come out. I left it in the end and took his bayonet."

"Much the same as me," I grunted. "I got Pigface. And I took his bayonet, too."

Don laughed. "Well, that's two of them at any rate. And two of the nastiest at that. Mac, boy, we're out! Do you realize it? We're out! We're free men!"

"I wouldn't crow yet. We're not out of the wood by a long chalk."

"Worst part's over though."

"I wonder."

There was a sudden rustling among the rubber trees to our left which started us running again. We were soon out of the small plantation and came to a wide stretch of secondary jungle, where the tall lalang grass reached up to our waists and sometimes to our chests. We had, so far, been moving due north; but I reckoned that to reach Rodriguez's house we needed to head somewhere between north and north-north-east.

"We'd better turn off to the right," I told Don. "Somewhere here we ought to hit the Bukit Timah Road."

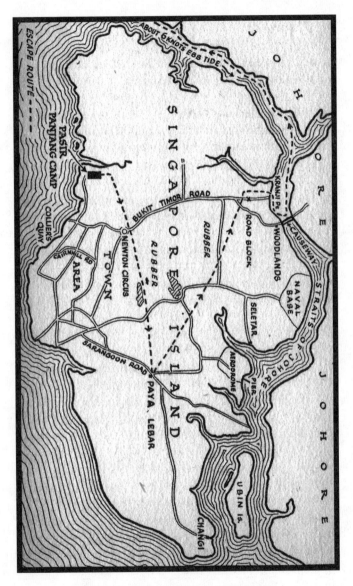

SINGAPORE: THE ESCAPE ROUTE

"You're the navigator, Mac. But I tell you, man, if your plotting's wrong, I'll send in a formal complaint to the Air Ministry when this little lot's blown over."

Partly by luck and partly by judgment, my navigation was dead accurate. We skirted through the outlying districts of Singapore where, if we were stopped by a Jap patrol, we hoped to pass as Eurasian (the north-eastern suburbs were full of Eurasians); then we came to a road—the Bukit Timah Road—and followed it for nearly a couple of miles. Once we tumbled hurriedly into the long grass as a party of Japanese soldiers went clumping by. We thought of keeping to the lalang grass; certainly it was tall enough to hide us, but as we brushed our way through it, it rattled and the noise seemed to us loud enough to wake the dead; so we went back to the road again. It was quite dark now. There was no sign of any of the others.

After about an hour we left the Bukit Timah Road, and struck into a wide belt of rubber trees which I knew stretched and sprawled for several miles almost up to the village of Paya Lebar.

It was dark and cool among the trees, but sweat was rolling off us as we moved warily through the endless succession of symmetrically planted estates, crouching low, gripping our bayonets, turning sharply at every suspicious sound, often diving for cover and lying motionless until we were satisfied there was no cause for alarm. The sky was cloudless and the bright twinkling stars acted as guides in our diagonal north-easterly trek. Behind us, towards the town of Singapore, hung belts of low mist lying in thin layers above swamp and jungle. Our impulse was to continue running and to reach Paya Lebar in the shortest possible time; but reason prompted caution; and the journey of only about eight miles took us more than six hours.

"Wonder where the others are," I whispered to Don as we scrambled along a rough track leading through thick, luxuriant foliage.

"Can't make it out," he whispered back. "We were almost last out through the gate; the others should be way ahead of us. Did you get hurt on the barbed wire?" he added.

"No—just a scratch or two. My shirt and shorts are ripped to pieces though. How about you?"

"Oh, I'm OK. My shirt's OK as well."

"Mustn't dirty your pretty silk shirt!" I gibed. Don was proud of his shirt.

It was close on midnight when I recognized the approach to Paya Lebar along the Yio Chu Kang Road. Once there had been a Naval WT Station here, not far from the southern perimeter of Seletar airfield. We moved cautiously through a maze of small intersecting tracks. Then out of the darkness loomed the great tree Rodriguez had said was less than fifty yards from his house; the moment we spotted it our feeling of tension increased. Squatting beside the track we discussed our next move.

"Now what?" asked Don. "Do we knock Rodriguez up or wait a bit for the others?"

"Better wait a bit," I advised. "I don't know about you, but I could do with a rest."

"Agreed," said Don. "We don't know what we may be in for."

So we lay side by side, stretched out on the grass by the huge bole of the tree, both of us were trembling and perspiring. After about twenty minutes, we heard a rustling in the trees behind us; we lay quite still, watching and listening. The noises grew more distinct—the snapping of twigs, the soft pad of running feet, then from beneath the heavy leaves emerged two crouched, bedraggled figures. Another pair had reached the rendezvous.

"OK, boys," I whispered, "take it easy." They dropped thankfully beside us.

By the bole of the tree we waited for nearly an hour. After ten minutes three more arrived; then a chap on his own; then another couple, and another, until at last there were twelve of us.

"Still five short," observed a tall young Scot.

We held a council of war. I ought perhaps to explain that, as we were a mixed party, composed of men and NCOs from all three Services and also civilians, it was difficult for any one of us to assume the role of leader. Donaldson and I had initiated the escape and, in the short time we were together, the others probably looked to us to take important decisions. We, for our part, thought it best only to outline a general plan of campaign and leave the others to follow on or not as they thought fit.

"I reckon we've waited long enough," I said.

"Sure," agreed Don, "We'll stay under cover; you call on our friend Rodriguez."

The others scattered into the bush as I slowly made my way, crouching low, towards Rodriguez's house. There was a door almost fronting onto the track, and a pale light streamed from the single open window. I knocked softly. There was no reply. I knocked again. There was a shuffling on the other side of the door, which opened a few inches.

Rodriguez, his face round and shiny, his eyebrows raised, and his forehead wrinkled, peered through apprehensively.

"It's me, McCormac."

"Come in." He opened the door just wide enough to let me through, then closed it quickly.

"How many got away?"

"Seventeen broke camp, but only twelve are here so far."

He shook his head; his eyes darted furtively around the untidy room. He looked scared out of his wits. His fear was infectious.

"Are there Japs about?"

"I don't think so. It's quiet enough." He looked at me unhappily. "Twelve's a lot for the boats."

"We can cross in relays. Where exactly are they?"

"Kranji Point, three hundred yards west of the Causeway."

"Good God, man, that's miles away!"

Rodriguez nodded. I saw the perspiration soaking through his singlet and his crumpled, threadbare slacks. He shifted uneasily.

"Yes, I know. That's the trouble."

There was a pause—an uncomfortable pause. He seemed to make up his mind quite suddenly.

"I can't go with you. I can't risk my family. You'll have to fend for yourselves."

I couldn't find it in me to quarrel with his decision. I knew as well as he did the sort of reprisals his family might expect.

"Can we use your boats?"

"Sure you can—don't worry about that. Do you know how to get there?"

I nodded, but as an afterthought asked him for details about the last few hundred yards. Then I smiled and patted his wet, podgy shoulder. "We'll be OK and thanks for all you've done." I turned towards the door, but he stopped me and pushed into my hand a wad of paper money—a thickish roll of Japanese dollars.

"Good luck," he whispered.

The door closed softly behind me.

I walked back to the tree, and the others, materializing out of the undergrowth, crowded eagerly around me. I found that another three escapers had arrived safely. We were still two short.

"Better wait for them, Don," I said. "We can't leave 'em on their own."

"OK."

"Anyone know what might have happened to them?" I asked.

A short, thickset civilian muttered that he thought a couple of chaps had fallen to the Japanese Tommy guns.

"How many Japs did we get?" Don asked him.

"Dunno. There were six or seven sprawled face down beside the guard house. It was all over too quickly to see much."

We waited about half an hour but the last two never came.

"They've had it," muttered Don. "Let's go."

We decided to make our way to the Causeway in groups of twos and threes, with about twenty yards between each group. Don and I were to lead the way, for I was in familiar territory and knew the roads and the best points at which to cross them. We were to regroup on the far side of the Naval Base Road, which led to the Causeway. The latter was the danger spot and was certain to be well patrolled and guarded.

We set off, Don and I in front, the next group some twenty-five yards behind, from which distance they could just see our shadowy figures moving cautiously from tree to tree. At first we kept to the welcome gloom of the rubber trees on the south side of the Yio Chu Kang Road. We passed the WT station, then a small burned-out village. There was no sign of life among the charred ruins. Then we came to a woodland area again, close to where I had joined the roadblocking party before Singapore had fallen: how many weeks ago ....

At last we reached the Naval Base Road, and saw at the bottom of it the twinkling lights of the Causeway over the Johore Strait. On the other side were the mainland, the hills, the jungle, the guerrillas. Our chance of freedom. Near the Causeway Don and I stopped among the twisted trunks and roots of the mangroves, waiting for the rest of the party to catch up. It was agreed that if we got across the strait we would again split into pairs and make our way independently towards the Kuala Lipis hills.

Once assembled we made a compact group and, bent low from the hips, we edged slowly forward across the mudflats towards the water, which we could hear lapping against the shore. The mudflats were slippery and quite devoid of cover. But there, thank God, drawn a little above the water's edge, were the two boats.

"Good old Rodriguez!" muttered a Welshman close behind me. "So, he played ball after all!"

"Shut up, you fool!" snapped Don.

Instantly all of us stiffened and froze motionless. Only ten yards away, dead in front of us, a number of dark figures were walking purposefully towards the boats. A Japanese patrol. Had we stood still and remained quiet, we might perhaps have got away with it. But from the rear of our party came a frightened yell.

"Japs!"

There were startled orders from the shadowy figures ahead, then the biting orange flashes of point-blank rifle fire. We had only one chance. Springing forward as one man, we rushed the patrol. Clubs and bayonets wielded by desperate men are terrible weapons. In a second we were among them, and a slithering mass of bodies fought savagely beside the quietly lapping water. I saw the white gleam of a Jap's teeth and, like a maniac, slashed my bayonet at his face. Together we dropped onto the mud and I felt him squirming beneath me, his nails tearing into my thighs. I changed my grip on the bayonet and using it like a dagger, stabbed it again and again into the writhing body clawing round my legs.

As suddenly as it had started, the fight was over.

Together with seven others I scrambled over the fallen bodies and rushed towards the nearest boat. A couple of Japanese fled in silent terror into the fringe of the mangroves. And seven of our party lay dead or dying on the wet, shining mud.

"Come on," someone muttered. "In a minute the swines will be swarming out."

There was just room for the eight of us in one boat, and this we together pushed and shoved down towards the water. It slid smoothly over the slime and mud and, once it was afloat, we tumbled in. The Welshman found a paddle lying in the bottom and with it he pushed off from the shore. He heaved hard, and the rest of us dragged our hands deeply through the water. Slowly—painfully slowly—we moved into the strait.

"How many dead!" muttered Don.

"Seven, I think."

"Only half of us left." The speaker was another Welshman: a

small, dark-haired man half-hanging over the gunwale. He was beating frantically at the water, using his hand as a paddle.

I looked round for oars or sail, but apart from the solitary paddle and a short stump of mast the bottom of the boat was almost empty. We tried paddling with our hands, using the paddle as a rudder, but seemed to make very little progress. In spite of our efforts we drifted eastward, parallel to the shore and towards the Causeway, only to turn northward at the last moment and again flow out to sea. As hard as we paddled to the northward we were carried towards the east, towards the Causeway, and the lights and the Japanese.

"Thank heaven it's dark," growled Don.

But it was not dark for long. Suddenly from the Causeway a searchlight flashed out brilliantly. For a few seconds it flicked on and off, then it steadied into a full broad beam, moving slowly in a golden pathway across the water. There was no escaping it. It was swinging in our direction.

"Down!" I hissed sharply.

Huddled on the floorboards below the level of the gunwale, we lay perfectly still. Suddenly the boat floated into light; light was all around us; and then it was dark again as the beam passed on.

"Don't move," muttered Son. "It'll be back."

It was. Again the pale golden light flooded over the boat; this time the beam steadied and remained trained on us. Every minute we expected to hear the rattle of machine-gun fire or the engine of an approaching launch. But after what seemed like hours, the light moved on and the boat was dark again.

Don peered over the gunwale. "Keep down, chaps," he ordered sharply.

There we lay, motionless and terrified, each of us feeling the adjacent bodies panting in and out, in and out.

"It's coming back again," he grunted. "Keep right down."

The searchlight played around us, like a cat uncertain whether the mouse is dead; then suddenly it cut off. As, with grunts and groans, we pulled ourselves up from our cramped positions, I saw that the scattered lights on the Causeway were much further away. We must have moved round with the current, have drifted up and parallel to the Causeway, and were now drifting away from it, westwards, out to sea.

"Not much point in trying to paddle," I said. "There's a five-knot tide here and it's taking us just about in the right direction."

"Thank God for that!" Don began to button up his shirt, for the night wind, striking off the water, was keen and chill.

It was reassuring to see the lights of the Causeway fading further and further into the distance, away into the milky haze of the horizon. All the same we were heading out to sea, out into the broad Straits of Malacca. I hoped that the tide would sweep us up the Malay Peninsula, and that, once we had drifted a fair way from Singapore, we would be able to paddle ourselves ashore into the mangrove swamps along the west coast of Malaya.

It was cold in the boat and none of us were wearing more than a tattered shirt, shorts and shoes. Our limbs were aching after the twelve-mile rush across the island from Pasir Panjang to the Causeway. Our bodies weren't used to that sort of exertion. My own legs were still smarting from the clawing scratches of the Japanese soldier, and congealed blood had thickened where the barbed wire had cut into my head and shoulders. We were a motley-looking crew, huddled closely together for warmth on the floorboards of the dilapidated twelve-foot boat. The Welshman was singing softly.

I crawled on hands and knees round the boat, taking stock of our few provisions. Up in the bows I came across a small drum of water, nearly full, also a few strips of dried fish and some rotten fruit. We shared the food round and half the water. There wasn't much for each man, but the water was nectar to us. Over the stern of the boat was a half-disintegrated covering of old and wispy straw, and under it a short mast. It was all sadly derelict, but the boat stayed afloat. I was dog-tired and, remembering that sleep had escaped me the night before, I nodded off with the others to the slight rhythmic pitching of the boat. Only the night before! Surely too much had happened, too quickly, for it to have been only yesterday morning that we were paraded between the atap huts of Pasir Panjang. It seemed impossible to believe that we were no longer prisoners, that this morning there would be no Jap guards to prod us into wakefulness, that there would be no barbed-wire cage around us—nothing but the open sea. The dawn, I thought, would find us free men.

The sun rose cold, fresh, and pink, its rays shafting flatly across the sea, whose grey surface caught and reflected in a myriad flashes the new light of day. Over to the east, several miles distant, was a thin pencil of land. We had drifted far. In the drum there were only a few inches of water. Though our tongues were beginning to feel thick and furry and our lips dry, we decided to leave the water and hold out as long as we could; for we knew the heat of day could bring terrors as great as, if not greater than the cold of night. But at first we found the sun's warmth on our stiffened bodies comforting as a hot bath in frosty weather. We took turns on the paddle, using our strength economically in an attempt to head the boat north-east towards the land. We made little progress. Then we tried paddling in unison with our hands; we moved with the élan of a water-flea crossing the Pacific. After an hour we gave it up.

"There's a slight breeze, Don," I said. "Let's tie our shirts together and try to rig up a sail."

We were just starting to peel them off when Don drew his breath in sharply.

"Hold it!" he snapped.

He pointed to the east and I followed the line of his finger towards the distant strip of land. There, low on the horizon, were two dots in the clear morning sky, becoming rapidly larger. Presently we heard the low hum of engines. Aircraft.

"Recognize 'em, Mac?"

"Not yet. They're fighters, I think."

The planes were low over the water and flying directly towards us. A quarter of a mile away they seemed to be head to the north of us; then one banked sharply towards us, followed immediately by the other.

"Look out!" I yelled. "They're Zeros."

"Overboard!" shouted Don. And he dived over the gunwale. In no time I was in beside him, and I remember my surprise at finding the water so warm. Three more of us jumped into the sea, but the others stayed crouched low in the bottom of the boat, their eyes following the aircraft as if hypnotized. The Zeros roared in only a few feet above us, then they climbed sharply until they were again mere specks in the sky. Then they turned in for the kill, sweeping down on the boat in a long shallow dive, their throttles wide open, little darts of flame spouting from the cannon at either wing-root. Those still in the boat tumbled over the side, one of them screaming "Watch out for sharks!"

I swam away fast and, as my ears filled with the roar of the fighters, took a deep lungful of air and dived under the water with all the power I could muster. I held my breath as long as I could and then, when the strain was at breaking-point, I surfaced like a fish thrown up by an underwater explosion. Behind me, the sea was churned up by cannon shells and the boat was upside down. I could see only three heads bobbing about in the fringe of the churned-up water.

"Look out, here they come again!" It was—thank God—an Australian voice: Don's. I dived again. Twice more the Zeros, cannon and machine guns blazing, swept down on the boat; then they circled low over the water. Finally they climbed high into the western sky and headed away up the Malacca Straits. I made sure they were out of sight before I swam back to the shell-holed keel of the boat, which was upside down but still floating. Don reached it just before me, and we clung on breathlessly, looking round at the foam-flecked waves for the other six. Only two heads appeared; and only two men, gasping for air, splashed their way over to my side of the keel and there sought a grip on the smooth, slippery wood.

"Let's turn it over," panted Don, and he swam over to our side.

The four of us trod water and heaved together until the boat rolled sluggishly over, bringing a mass of water inside it, so that the gunwale was only just above the surface. We were scared of sharks, and pulling ourselves into the boat, started to bale out furiously with our hands.

There was no sign of the others. Don and I watched anxiously for them, but the sea, apart from our riddled boat and the distant haze of land, was empty and devoid of any sign of lift.

I caught Don's eye.

"Sharks or bullets," I said.

So now we were four. Four out of seventeen. Two had died on the jungle fringe, breaking out from Pasir Panjang; seven more on the moon-lit mud close to Kranji Point; now another four had found their grave in the warm, untroubled waters of the Malacca Strait. We had covered perhaps twenty out of the two thousand miles to Australia; and, so pitiably soon, there were only four of us left.

Chapter Four

Besides Don and myself the other two survivors were a Welshman, whose name was Skinner, and a youngster who said his name was Roy.

Skinner—Skinny, as we all called him—was small, dark, profane and possessed of boundless energy and humour. An inveterate grumbler, he had a one-track mind and only one topic of conversation: women.

Roy was a very different character. He was tall, slightly built and softly spoken. A more reticent man I have seldom, if ever, met. Of his background we could learn nothing, and obviously his past life was something he did not wish to talk about. It was also obvious that he was ill, very ill, and that there was nothing much any of us could do to help him.

The four of us squatted on the bottom boards, water dripping from our clothes, baling out as fast as we could. We seemed to make little progress; after nearly ten minutes the boat still lay deep in the water, rolling slightly. I felt around for bullet and cannon holes under the water-level. Miraculously there seemed to be only two, and these I plugged by tearing strips off my shirt and wedging the sodden linen into the jagged cavities. We continued baling; and soon she was again riding smoothly.

"Leave a few inches of water on the bottom," said Don. "It'll help us keep cool."

He was wise.

I looked round for the water drum. It had gone; so had the food, so had the paddle, so had the mast. I lay back and thought, and the more I thought the more certain it seemed that we were going to die.

All that morning I watched the thin strip of land. Gradually, as the sun climbed high into the azure sky, the land began to disappear in an undulating haze of heat. And I knew that the tide was carrying us away from the Malayan coast, further and further into the open sea. It was a far cry now to the mountains of Kuala Lipis and the lush jungle that hid Rodriguez's guerrillas.

We lay in the open boat, broiling in the fierce tropical sun. The straw canopy had disappeared—disintegrated when the boat rolled over—and there was no shelter from the scorching rays. Side by side, we lay in the tepid water that lapped to and fro across the bottom of the boat.

"Like a lot of blinking haddocks coming to the boil," muttered Skinny.

I tried to lick my lips, and at once thought of the sheep's tongues that butchers sometimes display in their windows—big, fat tongues, swollen and roughened. That is how mine felt.

Hour after hour we lay there. We soon gave up talking, and drifted in apathy across the silent ocean, wondering how much longer we could hope to live.

By the evening all trace of land had disappeared. The sun slid slowly towards the horizon, then quickly dropped into the calm, iridescent sea, drenching the western sky in orange and crimson. Colour drained away from our world of sky and water, until only a deepening grey was left for reflection in the little undulation of the waves. The dark brought coolness to our bodies but no relief to our parched and swollen throats.

Hours passed. Gradually the stars were blotted out as from the north a dark mass of rain cloud spread across the sky. We watched it in an agony of hope. It was about midnight when the first soft droplets of rain pattered into the sea around us, bringing a cold smarting to our faces, which were burnt and tender from the sun.

"Rain, thank God," croaked Don; the rest of us were too far gone to speak, though I saw Roy's lips moving as though in prayer.

The first fine mist gradually gave way to a tropical downpour that lasted for close on an hour. We lay back, our faces turned towards the sky, our mouths wide open. We gulped down the water as it ran into our throats. Our torn clothing soaked up water; so we took off our shirts and laid them out on the gunwale so that they caught the rain on their spread surfaces. Then we wrung them out and drank. A little—but only a very little—we managed to save for the next day.

After the rain had eased off, we dozed fitfully, huddled back to back, the boat rocking gently in the swell of the open sea.

Dawn came. Another day, and we were still alone, riding the waves in a vast, horizon-to-horizon, empty world; like the first explorers on some strange and unknown planet. Hour followed hour, and as morning passed into afternoon we again felt that death was coming very near, creeping towards us over the flat, motionless sea.

There was no conversation, for we had no energy to talk. We

lay quietly, our bodies inert, our brains numbed, facing the approach of death with apathy. The sun climbed majestically and pitilessly above us. Was this to be the end? Flame and heat falling on us from the unknown sky—"that undiscovered country from whose bourn no traveller returns"? Was Pat a traveller there, too? Should I see her there? But how should I find her in the dizzy whirl of sun and shimmering heat? The sun hit me between the eyes, thumping at my forehead and shafting dull pain through the back of my head. My tongue was black and swollen and seemed to fill the whole of my mouth. The pulses throbbed in my neck, carrying drum beats to my ears and brain. There was no dignity in such a death as this.

The sun, our only companion throughout that long day, passed its zenith and fell again towards the western horizon. We judged it was about four o'clock when Skinny, who had been sprawled beside Roy on the bottom of the boat, jerked up his head. His eyes were glazed and staring. He had two front teeth missing, and when he spoke he whistled on his sibilants.

"Lithen," he lisped.

Very faintly, from somewhere in the north-western sky, there came the low and distant hum of aircraft.

"My God!" groaned Don. "Here they come again." Fearfully we stared over the gunwale, shielding our eyes against the sun's glare and searching the hazy sky above the horizon.

At last, low to the northward, we spotted a small, slow-moving dot.

"Looks like it's coming this way," I said.

In a few seconds there was no doubt about it; it was heading almost straight towards us.

"Only one this time."

"One's enough."

Our eyes were glued on the aircraft as it grew larger and gained definition. Undecided what to do, we could not summon up the strength to jump overboard again. What did it matter? Bullets were surely better than sharks or the agony of death from thirst.

I studied carefully the outline of the approaching plane. Memories of the silhouettes I had seen in the Operations Room at Seletar came flooding back to me.

"At least it's not a Jap fighter," I said. "It's a multi-engined job."

The plane was very near us now. I could see it was a flying boat. Then I recognized it.

"Good God! It's a Dornier!"

"A bloody Jerry?" muttered Roy.

"With a Jap crew, you bet your boots."

"May not be. The Japs have their own flying boats."

Skinny jumped to his feet, nearly upsetting the boat. Frantically he waved his arms. Then he stripped off his shirt.

"Let's wave!" he cried. "If they spot us, they'll pick us up. We'll have a chance with the Jerries."

Don pushed him down. "Pack it up, you fool, they'll only hand us over to the Japs."

But Skinny was not to be stopped. He leapt to his feet again, rocking the boat, and swung his shirt to and fro, up and down, above his head. He was shouting now, as if he really believed that the men in the plane could hear him. The big aircraft swept towards us, its engines roaring. It passed, at less than three hundred feet, only a few hundred yards ahead of us; then, in a few seconds it was gone, miles away towards the southern horizon.

"That's that," muttered Don.

I did not know whether I was glad or sorry.

"Look, look!" shouted Skinny. "It's turning!"

He was right. The aircraft banked slowly to starboard. Again it grew larger, and we could hear the noise of its engines increasing in volume until it thundered directly over the boat. Then it turned again, dipped a wing, went into a shallow dive and glided towards us; its engines idling, it landed only a hundred yards from our boat in a shower of glistening spray.

Skinny was beside himself with relief.

"Let's swim over to her," he screamed hysterically.

"Forgotten the sharks?" I asked him.

"Hang on, Skinny," said Don. "If they want us, they'll taxi over."

Hypnotized, we watched as the engines revved up and the flying boat approached us. We could see the oil-streaks from the engines under either wing; the rivets in the dull, grey-metal hull, and the faces vaguely staring at us behind the perspex of the cockpit. There was a quick burst from the engines and the aircraft drew alongside, its vast wing blotting out the sun. The hull scraped against the side of our boat, and I felt a mad desire to jump overboard: to swim as far away as possible from anything Japanese. The engines were ticking over slowly and the propellers fluttered in sporadic little bursts.

A door in the fuselage swung open and there, framed against the dark interior, stood a man: a white man. He was short, stocky and blond, dressed in white shirts and slacks. He was grinning broadly and shouted something in a guttural tongue. Above the coughing of the engines I caught only one word. It sounded like "Komm."

"Typical bloody Hun," grunted Don.

Skinny was the first to leave. With one foot on the gunwale, pushing it down almost below water level, he lifted himself on to an iron step that jutted out from under the open door. The man in white grabbed him by the arm and tumbled him into the plane. One by one we scrambled aboard, collapsing in a heap on the floor of the aircraft. At once the engines revved up, then roared to full crescendo. I saw the whipped-up water splashing against the perspex window. I felt the lift of the plane as she left the sea and soared up into the azure sky. Then a searing pain shot through my stomach, and I vomited against the metal side of the fuselage. I realized I had broken out in a cold, pricking sweat.

Two faces were staring down at me. One was the white man's, the other was a small delicately featured face; brown-skinned, not, I felt sure, the face of a Japanese. What could a brown-skinned man be doing in a German flying boat? For a second or two I could not take it in. Then, in a sudden flood of relief, I understood. I turned to the white man.

"Who are you?" I asked him in Malay.

"Royal Netherlands Air Force," he replied in Javanese—a tongue very akin to Malay.

I felt close to tears.

"It's OK, blokes." I was almost sobbing with relief. "They're not Huns and Japs. They're Dutch and Javanese."

Don, Roy and Skinny stared at me dumbly, then suddenly we all burst into excited talking; we were laughing and shouting at each other. In a minute we were all shaking hands. I turned again to the Dutchman.

"I am Royal Air Force," I told him. He grinned broadly.

The Javanese, who appeared to be the wireless-operator, disappeared for a minute; then he came back with steam mugs of coffee. We gulped it down like animals, and he filled our mugs again. Some cold rice and veal followed and, as I ate, I jerkily told the Dutchman our story. He smiled and beamed as he followed my narrative, but when I came to the end and tried, rather ineffectually, to thank him for picking us up, I noticed that he seemed worried and preoccupied. There was something going on, I felt, that I did not understand.

But Donaldson, munching food and swilling down his coffee, was impervious to any feeling of tension. He squatted against the fuselage muttering, almost to himself, "What a bloody miracle! What a bloody miracle!" Beside him, Roy was eating painfully and slowly; while Skinny was jabbering away in Welsh, chewing and talking so fast that pieces of food flew all around him. The aircraft, flying at its top cruising speed, dipped now and again in an air pocket. Under the stimulus of food and coffee, I began to feel better. I told the Dutchman he had saved our lives.

"Then I am glad we stopped for you," he said. "We didn't intend to at first. We're on a special job; but a sudden whim ..." he shrugged his shoulders, "... and back we came for you."

"A bloody miracle, a bloody miracle," Don was still muttering.

"Yes, miracle," I said to the Dutchman. "Where have you come from?"

"I cannot say," he murmured softly. Again the feeling of tension spread throughout the plane.

"Can you tell me where we are making for?" I asked.

"Yes, of course. A place near Medan in northern Sumatra."

"Thank God for that," Don cut in. "We can get in touch with our own troops there."

The Dutchman looked at us curiously.

"Sumatra has fallen," he said. "Didn't you know?"

Don's mouth gaped open.

"No," he grunted. "There weren't any papers in Pasir Panjang."

"I'm sorry," said the Dutchman.

"Then what are you going to do with us?" I asked him.

"We are landing a few miles from Medan. As far as we know there are no Japs in that area. We'll have to drop you there and leave you."

"Surely you can take us back," Skinny broke in. "Back to where you come from?"

"I'm afraid not. You see, we're on a special job, evacuating some people from Medan; a lot of very special people. We shall have to drop you, pick up the others and then return to our base."

"But you'll came back for us?" This from Skinny again.

"No. I am sorry."

We looked at each other. Our troubles, it seemed, were very far from over.

"Can you suggest some place we can make for?" Don asked.

"You might try to link up with the guerrillas; they're still fighting in the mountains in central Sumatra."

"Oh, Lord!" groaned Skinny. Don, his temper frayed, wheeled on him angrily.

"Well, so what? You'd prefer that to a boat in the middle of the sea, wouldn't you? Or perhaps you'd rather be in a Jap prison camp?"

"OK, OK. Take it easy," muttered Skinny.

Conversation lapsed as, in the gathering darkness, the Dornier flow steadily north-westward, heading for the north Sumatra coast.

It was dusk when we first sighted Sumatra, and quite dark when finally we touched down a hundred yards offshore. Through the windows of the aircraft we saw a great crowd of people, whites and Eurasians, emerging as if by magic from behind a dark line of mangroves; some of them were running along the shore gesticulating at the plane; others seemed to be holding back, as if afraid. Two of the Javanese crew inflated a rubber dinghy and ferried Don, Roy, Skinny and myself across the dark, softly breaking waters. Then they left us with a quick embarrassed goodbye as we clambered on to the featureless mudflats that ran along the shore between sea and mangroves. As we approached, the men and women held shyly back, but an old native stepped forward and greeted us. He was obviously a person of some authority. Bald and toothless, his old face—creased and wrinkled as if covered in soft, well-worn leather—broke in a crooked smile. He was dressed in a short sarong with the skirt drawn up between his legs like a toddler's napkins. He looked incredibly old. He motioned us to stand beside him in the shelter of the mangroves, a little aside from the others, and together we watched the Javanese aircrew ferry women and children over to the waiting flying boat. In all they made ten trips and I reckoned they took aboard almost sixty people. How they managed to squeeze them all in I cannot imagine. Then the engines, which had in the meantime been ticking over only enough to feather the propellers, jerked into life; for a few seconds, they exploded and backfired, then they echoed out in a deep, pulsating roar. From the pilot's cockpit a hand waved towards us in a last hurried farewell. Then the Dornier edged slowly forward; it gathered speed, the water curled away from the floats in twin wings of faintly luminous white; and at last, after a long bouncing takeoff, the place lurched into the air and roared away into the silent night.

Beside me Don sighed.

"They saved our lives, Mac. I suppose we shouldn't ask for more."

For several minutes, long after the plane had disappeared from sight, we stood beside the gently stirring mangroves, listening to the rhythmic engine-beat growing fainter. At last it died away, and we heard nothing but the rustling of mangrove leaves and the gentle lap of waves along an alien shore. Between us and Australia there still lay eighteen hundred miles of jungle and sea, not to mention several thousand Japanese.

Chapter Five

The old native, who had been watching us closely, now stepped forward and with a courteous gesture indicated that we were to follow him. He led us through the tangled mangroves into a lush hinterland of jungle; we stumbled wearily after him, our feet tripping over twisted roots and rotting tree stumps, our legs unwilling servants of our bodies. At last we came to a rough, beaten track. In our nostrils was the pungent tang of wood smoke. We were nearing a village.

After the excitement of the past few hours, the night without sleep, food or water, the days of exposure to the sun, the closeness of death, and the exhilaration of our rescue by the Royal Netherlands aircraft, I felt exhaustion seeping through my limbs and numbing my brain. I walked on in a sort of coma without thought or feeling. I glanced back at the others, who in the gloom were lurching along behind me like boneless india-rubber men. Roy, I noticed, was staggering more than the rest. Though tall, I noticed for the first time how slightly he was built; his sallow face was damp with an unhealthy sweat; only his stout heart and quiet determination kept him going with the rest of us. At Pasir Panjang, I remembered, he had been one of those badly hit by dysentery. I dropped back.

"In trouble, Roy?" I asked him.

"I'm OK Mac. Dysentery's doubling me up a bit, that's all."

"Do you want a hand?"

"No, it's OK, thanks."

But it wasn't OK; suddenly he lurched forward. Don and I took a grip on either arm and between us we helped him along.

We skirted round the first village and after about two miles of rough travelling through a dank world of rotting mangroves and stunted bamboo—the big flat leaves of pulpy vegetation slapping every now and then against our faces—we came to a kampong in a small marshy clearing. It was obviously built on the fringe of a swamp, for most of the atap huts were perched on poles and some of them stood in water. In the distance I caught the shimmer of moonlight reflected on the still surface of a lake. I had no idea where we were, apart from the fact that I knew Medan to be in north-eastern corner of Sumatra; as far as I could remember most of the country there consisted of low-lying mangrove swamps and small inland waterways.

The old native halted and approaching one of the huts gestured us to follow him up the steps, constructed crudely out of a tree trunk. We groped our way into the dark interior where, almost at once, we collapsed on the rush-strewn flooring, overcome by the unfamiliar feeling of security. The old man smiled at us, as a father might smile on his children when they come home weary from play; he lit a small oil lamp, and bade us rest and remain where we were until morning. We lay back in the long shadows cast by the lamplight, four weary, skinny, emaciated figures; we luxuriated in the heaven-sent comfort. The old man left us. Presently he returned, and with him were two women, one with a huge jar of water and the other with a dish of food. Greedily we gulped the water down—the woman had to leave us three times to refill her jar—and afterwards, with equal greed, we attacked the food. None of us knew or cared what food it was. Basically it was rice, and it was warm and palatable. We ate and ate—far more than our stomachs could comfortably stand. Not a word was spoken. The native and the women stood watching us, the women coming forward to ladle more food into our rough bowls as we finished each helping. Don did not finish his. He fell asleep as he was eating, sitting cross-legged with his bowl of rice in his lap and his wooden spoon held limply between his fingers.

In Malay I thanked the old man for his kindness and asked him to forgive my friend's bad manners.

"It does not matter," he said quietly. "You have eaten and now you must sleep."

With a parting smile, his stubble of whiskers showing white against the darkness of his face, he left us. The two women bowed slightly to us, then they followed the old man. I heard the soft pad of their feet descending the worn steps of the tree trunk, then I stretched out, my head cupped in my palms; within a minute I was fast asleep.

It was a long sleep, deep and untroubled.

Skinny was the first to wake—or so he told us afterwards—but even he did not stir until a little before noon. By himself he had a look round the kampong, then he came back to the hut and waited for us to rouse one by one. When I awoke, he was squatting on his haunches, staring through the doorway at the bright shafts of sunlight, while Don was curled up, childlike in his sleep, with his arms flopped over his eyes.

"Where's Roy?" I spoke softly, anxious not to disturb Don.

Skinny thumbed towards the doorway and with his other hand patted his stomach; he drew up his mouth significantly.

I nodded. Presently there was a slow tread up the steps and Roy crawled in, his face white and drawn.

"Dysentery?" I asked him.

"Too damned true!"

He dropped into a corner of the hut, curled up again and fell into a troubled sleep. Several times that afternoon Roy had to leave the hut, each time returning paler and weaker, so that by the evening he scarcely had strength enough to pull himself up the tree-truck steps. And he wasn't the only one. Whatever it was—dysentery, diarrhoea or colic—we all had repeatedly to descend the steps, nearly doubled up with sharp spasms of cramp in our stomachs. Starved for weeks in the privation of the camp at Pasir Panjang and then in the open boat, our stomachs revolted against the mass of food we had eaten the evening before. As one after another we staggered out to relieve ourselves in the fringe of the jungle, only a few shafts of sunlight threaded their way through the thick matted foliage above us, and the vegetation below flourished thick, spongy, green and obnoxious in a clammy greenhouse heat.

That evening we sat in the hut and tried to work out exactly what we should try to do. Clearly, we could not stay long in the kampong; that would be unfair to our native hosts. It was also clear that Sumatra was completely in the hands of the Japanese and we were bound to meet them whichever way we went. North of Sumatra was Sabang, jumping-off ground for the Indian Ocean and the Nicobar Islands. But we had no boat and our memories of the Indian Ocean were far from happy. To the west lay the mountains. To the east was the sea, the Malacca Strait and beyond it Malaya. South was Lake Toba and its surrounding fever-ridden marshlands. Between us and Java was a distance of more than eight hundred miles.

The more I thought about it, the surer I felt that westward to the mountains offered our only hope. I discussed it with the others.

"If we head west towards the mountains," I argued "we might be able to link up with guerrillas. There should be fewer Japs there than anywhere else; and again it will be cooler in the hills. Once there we can take it easy and try to get some of our strength back."

"OK by me," said Don. "Maybe we can even make Australia that way."

"Some hope you've got," chimed in Skinner. "Australia's out of your life, cobber, for the next few years."

"What do you think, Skinny?" I asked him. "Are you for the mountains too?" Roy was asleep and well out of the conversation.

"OK by me," he answered. "I'll tag along with you. I haven't a clue where we are. And anyway you know the ropes better than I do."

"Too true," cut in Don.

"Just think," Skinny went on, not in the least put out. "A few months ago I was safe an' sound in Cardiff. Now look where I've landed up!"

"I reckon you'd better forget Cardiff," I said quickly. "I reckon we'd all better put our old lives right out of our minds. What are we? To the Japs, and to all intents and purposes, we're dead. If we start thinking back, we'll stir up memories that'll drive us mad. We've no homes now. No past. It's going to be a day-to-day fight just to stay alive. Our only chance is to concentrate on one thing only—just staying alive—that and nothing else."

But Pat's smiling face swam before me, even as I spoke.

"That's the gen," said Don. "Away with sentimentality."

I caught the note of irony and looked at him closely. Don wasn't the sort of man who wore his heart on his sleeve. But that by no means meant he hadn't got one. I was never quite certain of Don.

I wasn't certain about Skinner, either—but in a different way. Skinner, for all his flashes of wit, was often morose and surly. He seemed to have a chip on his shoulder—apparently he couldn't forgive his unit for leaving him stranded in Malaya—"They never bloody well waited for me," he had said. Also I hadn't liked the way I'd seen him eyeing the native women. Skinny might, I thought, well prove to be a nuisance.

"Look," I said. "I can speak Malay and I've had some experience of the jungle. I used to travel about a bit during my leaves. Can I offer myself as the party's spokesman and guide?"

Don looked at me curiously and wiggled a finger in his ear.

"You're a queer cove, Mac," he said. "You offer yourself as spokesman and guide. Who the hell else do you think could manage to see us safely through? We'll do as you say, but if your navigation goes astray, I know what I'll do when this lot's over."

"What?" I asked.

"Write a letter of complaint to the Air Ministry," he grunted.

"You've said that before," I grinned at him. "Think of something new, cobber."

Don glanced sourly at me, then he too broke into a grin.

Presently the two women who had brought us food the night before mounted the steps in the tree trunk. Again they carried a jar of water and four bowls of steaming rice. Roy wasn't able to touch his, and Don and I ate a little only because we didn't want to hurt the feelings of our hosts. Skinny, however, ate his bowlful voraciously. When we had finished, I thanked the women, who smiled at us and withdrew.

"I hope these jokers aren't fattening us up for the kill," said Don. He knew as well as I did that the unwritten law of the East forbade any villager to turn away a starving stranger. We also knew that the same unwritten law did not forbid him afterwards to knife his guest to death.

It was nearly dark when the old native again came into the hut and offered us cigarettes (bitter, potent and narcotic). We all accepted one, except Roy. Then the old man sat on his haunches and told us how pleased he was to entertain us and how happy he would be to look after us as long as we stayed in his kampong.

"But," he added, "you must not be here many days."

"Why not?"

"The Japanese might come again. Already they have been here once."

I questioned him about the people we had seen boarding the flying boat.

"Tuan," he said, "we had been hiding them and feeding them for many weeks—ever since the wireless told us the Japanese had captured Java."

Don and I exchanged glances. So Java too had fallen.

"You have a wireless, then?" I asked.

"Not now. The tuan who was here last night told us to smash it."

"What tuan was that?"

"A Company man. He came with many others—men, women and children. All day he sat with his wireless. Yesterday afternoon he told us we must have the people ready to go into a great boat. Then when the flying boat came, the tuan left with the others, and before he went he smashed his wireless set."

"Was it a big wireless?" I asked him.

He showed me the size with his hands.

"Obviously a transmitter," I muttered to Don. I turned again to the old native.

"Where are the broken pieces?"

He shrugged his shoulders and looked away. It was clear that he would say no more about the radio.

"Where are the Dutch and British troops?" I asked him. "Are there any near here?"

"I do not know, tuan. Many troops were in Medan a little time ago."

"How far is it to Medan?"

"About two days' walking from here."

"Are there many Japanese there?"

"I do not know. But some of our men will be back from Medan this night. They will tell us everything."

I interpreted his news to the others. Roy was awake now and looking better; there was more colour to his cheeks.

"Old man," I went on, "if you were us, which way would you travel?"

"Towards the setting sun, tuan."

"To the west. Are there many soldiers there?"

He did not answer, and after a moment's silence I went on.

"Why can't we stay here; live with you, catch our own fish to eat and wait until our soldiers come back?"

"Tuan, we are only a small village and there are hardly enough fish for ourselves. If you stay, you will bring us trouble."

"Then we will leave as soon as possible," I told him. He brightened instantly.

I asked him if he would tell me a little of the customs of the Sumatran people so that on our way to the mountains we could ask for help and not, through ignorance, offend our hosts. He promised he would. He promised, in fact, to help us in any way within his power; provided we would not stay long.

"Can't say I blame him for telling us to clear out," Don commented when I told him the position. Indeed none of us thought of blaming him.

I went across to the hut entrance with the old man. As he climbed down the steps, I could see the little concourse of native men, women and children staring up at us from below. I waved to them and indicated the doorway, inviting them to come and talk to us. One or two did, and stood on the top steps watching us curiously. Roy squatted on his haunches, Don leant against one of the rough wooden walls, Skinny grinned at the native women, eyeing them up and down, while I tried, without much success, to talk to them. They were solemn and a little scared at first—tiny, brown-skinned people with soft, dark eyes and red, betel-stained teeth. When I spoke to them in Malay, they giggled, came forward and tried to touch me with tentative, half-frightened fingers.

Throughout the day, in between our hurried exits to the jungle fringe, we held court to the children of the kampong, and gradually they became less frightened and more playful. We were fed on chicken and rice, durians and turtle eggs. We agreed among ourselves to prolong our stay as long as possible—a week if we could manage it—so as to build up strength to face the hardships which we knew must lie ahead. That night we dropped off to sleep early, while it was still light, contented in mind, relaxed in body, and caring little for the mosquitoes that hummed and pinged around us long after we had turned out our solitary oil lamp.

We stayed in and around the hut for three more days, resting and regaining our strength. On the afternoon of the third day the old native came to us again. He looked anxious.

"Tuan, you must leave at once."

"Why?"

Impassively, he produced a circular printed in Malay and Dutch.

"Tuan, our men brought this with them when they returned from Medan last evening."

I glanced at the small printed leaflet. "The Emperor of Japan," I read, "the Son of Heaven, has declared that the peoples of Asia have suffered too long under the heels of their European masters. The peoples of Sumatra, whatever their calling, are equal to the white men and, although the white man had many guns and they, the Sumatrans, had none, Japan has sent her bravest soldiers to help overcome the white men." The leaflet—like an election manifesto—went on with promise after promise. The natives could look forward to lives of ease and plenty though the way would be hard. Meanwhile they must all cooperate and work towards coprosperity, no matter how much temporary suffering might result. It was all for their ultimate good. The real point of the leaflet was saved up for the last paragraph. Four hundred guilders were offered for information given to local Japanese commanders of the whereabouts of white men or their friends.

I translated it for the others.

"Saucy sods," grunted Skinny. "I'm worth more than four hundred guilders."

Don eyed him doubtfully. "Only as dog's meat," he said.

"Shut up wrangling, you two." I turned to the old man, as he spoke almost pleadingly.

"Tuan, it grieves me much that you should have to leave," he said. "You have eaten in my house. You are as one of us. But I cannot vouch for all the people in my village. We are poor people and four hundred guilders is a fortune. It would be best if you left at once."

I reassured him. "We will go then. But can you first give us food that we can take with us and parangs in case we are attacked?"

He bowed and smiled, relief showing clearing on his face. "Surely, tuan, I will give you all you want."

I turned to the others. "Well, this evening we'll be off again. Australia here we come ..."

We spent the rest of the day, helped by the native women, patching our worn footwear and tattered clothes. We had only our shirts, singlets and shorts, and they were torn and filthy. The women took the clothes away and, after mending the largest tears, washed them in the nearby lake; they dried quickly in the hot midday sun. We reinforced our shoes with stout bark which we cut into leather-like strips and bound in broad ribbons round the soles and uppers. Our hair and beards were still thick, but during the afternoon Don and I shaved and cut each other's hair. Then, looking comparatively smart and clean, we borrowed a knife from one of the natives, went into the jungle, and hacked off and trimmed a couple of stout four-foot staves.

All of us felt a great deal better after our three restful days, much of which we had spent sleeping; and even Roy had lost his drawn, haggard look, although he was still troubled by dysentery. Skinny was bearing up well and seemed to be in better physical condition than any of us—with his spare wiry body the heat troubled him little; but he was temperamental, a man of quickly changing moods—sometimes grumbling and morose, sometimes high-spirited and full of fun.

Shortly before dusk the old native climbed up the steps into the hut. He was laden with food, wrapped in moist, thick leaves the villagers had picked from the surrounding jungle. Most the food was a mixture of cooked rice and crushed prawns, not very palatable, but full of nourishment. He handed each of us two parcels of food and a parang, and solemnly wished us all in turn good luck, good health and a good journey. While he spoke, he insisted that we ate a last bowlful of rice and chicken handed round by two women. He said that we should reach the mountains in six or seven days, and again explained the rough track we should follow.

When finally we descended the steps, a far fitter-looking quartet than when we had arrived, it seemed that every man, woman and child in the kampong had turned out to bid us goodbye. They surrounded us excitedly, shouting and waving, as the old man led us out along a track leading to the west. We looked back towards our hut, nostalgic already for the comfort of its roof and the security of its position in the centre of a friendly kampong. One by one the villagers dropped behind as the old native led us down a clearly defined track through the jungle; at last he stopped, his toothless gums showing in a broad, beaming grin. Each of us shook him by the hand and patted him on the back (a procedure which seemed to delight him), then, alone, we headed westward through dense steaming jungle towards the mountains we could not as yet even see.

By tacit agreement I led the party, my parang stuck in the belt of my shorts, and under my arm the parcels of precious food.

For the first twenty minutes we padded along in silence towards the setting sun, now low in the western sky. We were a quiet, subdued party. Each of us realized that now, once again, we were on our own, and the reality of what we were facing up to—a sixteen-hundred-mile trek to freedom through Japanese-held jungle—was only just coming home to us. Our escape would be both a battle of wits in avoiding the Japanese and at the same time a test of physical endurance. If our wits failed us, we should be caught by the Japanese and death would come to us in some remote guard hut or prison camp. If our endurance failed us we should die in the vast remoteness of the jungle, unheeded and alone. But at least we had a chance. The jungle could be a friend as well as an enemy: it could hide us and provide our food and water; or just as easily it could kill us. Ours would be a battle for survival against both man and nature; and it seemed to me that the Japanese might well prove less dangerous than the jungle, with its kraits (a little black and gold snake some eighteen inches long and thick as an index finger), scorpions, poisonous spiders, and malaria-carrying mosquitoes; not to mention its humid heat, lack of food and occasional lack of water. And the distance to Australia was sixteen hundred miles.

The track curved away in front of us, in and out of enormous trees, with trunks three or four feet thick, that soared up and away into a roof of thick foliage, boughs and creepers. We were in a dark, lofty tunnel that wound its way over the slippery mud and earth. Only a few shafts of sunlight filtered through the tangle of vegetation, and lit up the gently rising mist in slanting bands of pale-gold light. We were bewildered by the vastness of the jungle, its hypnotic, sensuous strength. It was to us, that first day, like some evil creature, alive and malignant, watching our every move.

Sweat soaked over us; soon our thin shirts and shorts were clinging to us like sodden paper; breathing was like inhaling vapour in a Turkish bath. We padded along, at five-yard intervals, keeping a wary eye on the track ahead and to the rear and also on every creeper and bush that overhung it.

About a mile from the village I decided to call a halt. The others came panting up behind me.

"What's up, Mac?"

"Nothing much, except this awful heat. But I reckon we might lay up awhile here, in case our friends from the kampong have told the Japs to expect us. Don't forget we're worth four hundred guilders apiece."

"Damned good idea," muttered Don, smoothing the sweat away from his forehead with the back of his hand. "But what a suspicious man you are!"

We waited for nearly a couple of hours. Nothing happened, except that Skinny and Roy began to show increasing signs of nervousness; they kept starting up and peering into the jungle through the immense flat leaves of the tree under which we were hiding.

"First false alarm," said Skinny. "Let's get going. This place gives me the creeps."

"Better careful than sorry," growled Don.

We started off again, but by now the sun had sunk low; its rays glinted fitfully through the tangled trees and painted the undergrowth with spattered colour; a mosaic of green, grey and gold. Our track was well defined, but in the increasing gloom we began to tread more warily, uncertain whether the curling shapes beneath our feet were tree trunks or snakes; then we heard with mounting anxiety an increasing number of unexplained noises from either side of the track.

Don caught up with me. "Getting a bit tough, isn't it?" he panted.

"I reckon it is. There's no point in breaking our necks. Let's call it a day."

The others at once cheered up.

"Fair enough," said Don. "We've all our lives in front of us."

Roy and Skinny burst out laughing, a shade hysterically I thought.

"All our lives in front of us!" cackled Skinny. "Forty years in the jungle. Christ, what a lovely thought!"

We groped our way off the trail and after some twenty yards came to a cluster of small, closely grouped trees with low-hanging branches; here we made a shelter by hacking away the thick grasses from underneath the huge, fern-like leaves. Our parangs cut cleanly at first but blunted quickly.

"How about a fire?" suggested Don.

"No, do," I said. "No matches."

"Try rubbing two boy scouts together." This, of course, was

Skinny.

We all cackled with laughter, and with a rattle of wings and an angry scream a parrot-like bird flashed out of the tree above our shelter. We leapt to our feet. Our nerves were all on edge.

"No fire," I said sharply. "It might attract the Japs. You three stay here; I'm going to have a look round."

As I ducked out of the shelter I heard Skinny grumbling away that a fire would scare off the "bleedin' jungle monsters", then I was alone, outside the shelter and beneath the low-branched trees. They were growing on the edge of a small clearing. I skirted around the open space, then forced my way through the thick, tangled grasses back to the trail. I walked down it some thirty yards, then struck off towards the shelter, approaching it from a slightly different direction. It was well hidden, and I had some difficulty in finding it again.

"No need to keep watch," I said when I rejoined the others. "We're well tucked away, and the jungle hides us from the track."

"This blinkin' jungle," muttered Skinny. "It'll be the death of me. All I've seen of jungle up to now is the football ground at Cardiff."

"Ease up on Cardiff," grunted Don, "or I'll start on Darwin."

We unwrapped some of our food and ate about a third of it. Then we lay down on the soft, moist earth. Thirst began to nag us, for we had no water. The old native had told me we would before nightfall come to a series of streams and trusting his word we had brought no water with us. We had now no alternative but to wait for the morning when we could search for the streams, or at least lick dew off the leaves.

"Are we all sleeping in here together?" asked Roy.

"Yes," I said, "I reckon so."

"Well, keep your side of the bed," piped up Skinny. "If anyone tries to make a pass at me, I'll scream the jungle down, and tell me mother in the morning."

"Wrap up, for Pete's sake," muttered Don.

"Sure, that's just what I'm going to do," grinned Skinny, draping an assortment of fern leaves over his spindly legs. He had, always, to have the last word.

Night brought utter darkness in place of the twilight gloom; but the less we could see the more we imagined; and our nerves tautened in the shelter and fear was our acknowledged guest. From the edge of the clearing a piercing scream tore across the silence. Skinny leapt to his feet, his eyes staring. I felt the hair rising on the nape of my neck. Suddenly I realized what it was.

"OK, OK, it's only a monkey."

More screams echoed across the clearing, ending in a thin, angry chattering; for a long while there was silence. About an hour later we heard a swift rustling in the undergrowth outside the shelter; a rustling that ended as suddenly and unexpectedly as it had begun. Later in the night we heard other sounds: a heavy crashing through the trees, followed by the soft slither of a crawling reptile. When it was quiet, I lay awake, wondering what was coming next. Most of the time the others were awake, too. The suspense and tension of that terrible night tattered our nerves. Now and then one or another of us would doze off fitfully, only to be woken stiff with discomfort, tormented by thirst, as some terrifying sound broke through the curtain of sleep.

The dawn was never more welcome.

As none of us had slept for more than a few hours we decided to travel only till noon, then rest and start our journey again at night.

That morning our most pressing need was to find water, and luckily less than a mile down the trail we came to several small streams. At the first one we splashed cold water over our heads and shoulders, cupped our hands in the clear, swift-moving water and drank our fill. Afterwards we washed thoroughly and sat down to eat another third of the food we had brought with us from the kampong. Then, refreshed, we again followed the trail along the northern slope of a straight, shallow valley.

Towards midday the jungle began to thin a little and we found ourselves, still heading west, in more open terrain of shrub and bamboo with the hot sun striking through occasionally. The trail here was less well-defined and we decided to halt as planned for a sleep, each of us making his own shelter, about thirty yards apart from the others, so that if one were spotted the rest would have a chance of getting away. But still we could not sleep. It was too hot.

Skinny and I soon abandoned our hideouts and looked around for food. After about ten minutes I spotted a thick, tangled vine, studded with what looked like coarse, hairy chestnuts. I recognized them as rambutans. I gathered as many as I could stuff into my shirt and the pockets of my shorts—they pricked annoyingly against my skin—and took them back to the others, explaining how to split and crunch the nuts, which tasted surprisingly sweet—like a mixture of fruit juices. Don found a bush bearing large berries which looked like a prickly pear. I had never seen quite this variety before though I recognized the general species. However, we noticed the birds eating them, so I peeled the skin off and risked a nibble at the soft pulp inside.

"Tastes OK," I said. "Usually if the birds eat it and it tastes all right, a berry should be safe enough."

So we each ate a handful of the large, greenish berries. They had an acid tang but were not unpleasant and helped to ease our thirst.

My shoes were becoming quite a problem. The soles, despite the first aid I performed on them back at the kampong, were peeling away and the uppers were badly split. I decided there and then to cut them up, keep the strips of leather as a reserve and walk barefooted—a rash decision as I discovered later when we took to the trail again at sundown. It wasn't so much that the soles of my feet became sore and bruised—for they quickly healed—but the calves of my legs began to ache unbearably.

Nevertheless, in the gathering darkness we again plodded on. Soon the track led back to the jungle and there the twilight chorus of birds and animals began again, shattering the still, humid air. Skinny began to sing some fervent Welsh air.

"Shut up!" snapped Roy and Don together.

Skinny muttered something unintelligible and stopped.

Ducking under loose creepers and sagging branches, we stumbled along, now and then losing the trail altogether.

After about two miles I called a halt.

"There's no future in this," I said. "Let's chuck in for tonight and start again in the morning."

The others agreed readily. This time we made a more elaborate shelter about forty yards from the track and settled down for the night on the damp, spongy earth. I hoped that now the jungle was losing a little of its unfamiliar terror, we should get a good night's rest. But it was not to be. After only about twenty minutes a sharp, piercing scream from Skinny jerked us into terrified awakeness. He was flailing about on the ground, his arms and legs thrashing into the foliage of the shelter.

"A snake!" he screamed. "I've been bitten!"

As we crowded round him, Donaldson gave a gasp of gear.

"Crikey, it's got me too!"

I moved instinctively away to the far side of the shelter. Then I too felt a sharp stab in my leg, followed by another on my shoulder. In the darkness, the three of us thrashed panic-stricken, in a confused mêlée. I felt another stab on my thigh, and slapped my hand down hard. Something small and hard squirmed and struggled through my fingers. I caught it and, as best I could in the darkness, looked at it closely. It was an ant but what an ant! A huge, vicious-looking insect, a full half-inch long.

"It's OK," I said. "They're only ants."

There were hundreds of them swarming round the damp earth and crawling up our legs. We had built our shelter almost on their nest. Quickly snatching up our food and parangs we scrambled out into the still, silent jungle. The tall trees, their upper branches merging into the night sky, seemed to be watching us malignantly.

Once again we stumbled along the trail, myself in front, Skinny and Roy next, and Don bringing up the rear. We agreed to push on a few hundred yards then look for another place to camp; but after only a couple of minutes, my foot sank deep into soft, slimy mud. I had to jerk back hard to pull it out. Unable in the dark to see what was happening, Skinny and Roy piled up behind me, cursing saltily, and Don, thinking we had met a Jap patrol, ducked swiftly into the undergrowth.

"Swamp," I said. "We can't cross this tonight."

Don emerged from his hideout.

"Phew, it stinks," he muttered. "Let's go back."

"What, back to them ants?" wailed Skinny. "Not bloody likely."

I looked around me. "There's only one thing for it," I said. "We'll have to spend the night in a tree. We'll be all right if we climb about ten feet and wedge ourselves in a fork. We can wrap ourselves up in creepers."

The others seemed doubtful; but I found a suitable tree and scrambled up to a huge branch that was about three feet thick where it joined the trunk. While the others watched from below I wedged myself tightly in and pulled over me festoons of a small-leafed creeper. The bark felt cool and spongy, coated with a thick velvet moss. It was surprisingly comfortable.

"Night night," I called down. "Tea and biscuits at seven-thirty."

The others grunted, then one by one pulled themselves up on to branches similar to mine. There was an occasional smothered curse or a quick scrape of a foot against the trunk until they had all wedged themselves in. Then we were quiet. The last I remember before I dozed off was Don's lazy Australian drawl, "Just like a lot of ruddy chooks roosting."

That night we slept surprisingly well. Often, half-asleep, half-awake, I twisted myself into a more comfortable position and twice I nearly toppled out when the screech of some jungle creature awakened me with a jerk. Very early in the morning there came from the base of my tree a strange, high-pitched clucking, followed by a low growl and the scraping of claws against the bark. Then it was quiet.

I was awake when dawn spread its first grey fingers of light over the jungle. Looking around, I saw the others, crooked up in sleep, their limbs in fantastic twisted positions. I must have dozed off again, for later I woke to see Don was staring across at me.

"What ho, cock," he said cheerfully. "What do we do now? Crow?"

One by one we scrambled down. Each of us had slept better than in the shelter, and feeling both cheerful and refreshed, we again headed westward along the narrow trail. It was not of course long before we came to what I thought was a swamp. But it was more than a swamp; it was a vast stagnant lake stretching away, dark and evil-smelling, into the overhanging vines. A swirl in the water, only a few yards to our right, made us turn quickly. Then we froze.

"Look," said Skinny. "A croc!"

Suddenly, having seen the one, we noticed others; dozens, if not hundreds, of them, lolling idly in the green, scum-surfaced water, or crawling on muddy claws up the shallow sloping mudbanks. They had wicked, heavy-lidded eyes.

"No wonder the place stinks," said Don. "Let's get out of this."

I looked at the stagnant pools of water, at the tangle of vine and creeper that fringed the water's edge, and at the thin coils of mist rising slowly into the humid air. A few days of this, I thought, and we'll be down with malaria. I agreed we should turn back.

"But the track seems to go on," pointed out Roy. "And it wasn't very overgrown."

We tried to follow the track, but after a few yards lost it and were hopelessly bogged down.

"Damn this," said Don, floundering up to his knees in green, stagnant water. "Let's get the hell out of this."

"Just like a blinking film," Skinny grumbled as we headed back along the track. "Can't you imagine it? 'With Skinner through the Sumatran jungle!' Tom-toms and music, natives waving spears a-whooping round a lovely white girl lashed to a tree. I can just see her heaving bosom. In comes Skinner, pith helmet on his head, a Colt in either hand. He throws himself on the girl ..."

"Oh, shut up, you randy bastard," snapped Don.

Skinny muttered angrily.

We took a rough bearing and decided to head south, parallel to the swamp; every now and then we would, we agreed, strike off to the west and see if the swamp could be skirted. To our left the country was fairly open, with tall, spiky grass broken here and there with clumps of stunted bamboos. This was no good to us; we could too easily be seen. To our right was the jungle; this suited us better, and we kept close to its fringe.

My feet were giving me trouble; the cuts and scratches were festering and swelling up. Soon we came to a stream where we drank deeply and I bathed my feet, afterwards tearing the sleeves from my shirt and using them to wrap round my feet as bandages. Skinny and Don were in good physical condition, but Roy was weak from dysentery. Already, after only two days, we had begun to look like a company of ape-men—scraggy, bearded creatures, with wild eyes, thick, matted hair and bare, scabby legs.

For most of that day we walked southward along the jungle fringe, and estimated that by nightfall we had covered over seven miles. This was our second complete day after leaving the kampong.

For five more days we continued on the same southerly course. Every afternoon we struck hopefully westward, but came each time to the same impenetrable belt of swamp. In the far distance to our right was the deep blue and purple of the mountains. To our left, the open grassland stretched to the eastern horizon. We made no desperate effort to penetrate the swamp as the going was comparatively easy, but continued along the jungle fringe. Occasional streams provided water for drinking and bathing, and we fed off berries, fruit (mostly durians) and edible roots. After a couple of days I was able to discard the bandages round my feet, and my soles grew tougher with each mile we walked until soon a leathery pelt formed where there had before been only soft sensitive skin. The others, still in their dilapidated shoes, envied me. Sometimes we skirted round a kampong—primitive little villages made up of a few clustered atap huts. We always avoided the inhabitants. Since we needed no help, it seemed foolish to risk showing ourselves. Each of us carried a reserve of fruit and yams tied together in a bundle made out of his shirt or shorts. It was I who started this fashion. One particularly humid afternoon I took off my shorts and wrapped the bandage from my feet around my loins. By tying the two trouser-legs together the shorts made a useful carrier bag. Skinny and Roy followed suit, though they had to tear strips from off their shirts in lieu of bandages. Don, always proud of his smart silk shirt, was reluctant to follow our example, but he gave way in the end.

And so, day after day, we loped along, usually in line one behind the other, until on the sixth day the grassland gave way to a more wooded type of country, and by the evening we again found ourselves hemmed in by thick, humid jungle; Don and I climbed the tallest tree we could find to survey the way ahead, but as far as we could see there was nothing to the south and west but a vast expanse of jungle. There was no alternative but to plough our way through it. It was, we soon found, a peculiar stretch of jungle; for at night (usually much noisier than the day) there was a brooding and sepulchral silence. It was peculiar too because, although the tall trees grew thickly overhead and quite shut out the sun, the vegetation underneath was thin, rotting and lifeless. The rough track we were following was soft and soggy beneath our feet. With each pace I took ooze squelched in between my toes.

"Another damned swamp," said Roy.

"How right you are," Don agreed. "It stinks like hell. The sooner we're out of this the better."

"It's like a queer dream," murmured Skinny. "Or perhaps I'm dead and didn't qualify for the golden gates."

Silently in single file we pushed into the cathedral-like gloom. At first we expected, any day, to see the trees ahead thinning out. But eventually we became reconciled to walking for ever in the silence and the green half-light between primeval trees. It took us thirteen days to cross that terrible jungle. Day after day we plodded along, sweating in our thin shirts, sometimes losing the indeterminate southern trail in the dense, matted undergrowth and scrambling about in panic until we had found it again; at night we were plagued by mosquitoes and insects; we bathed and drank in vile stagnant pools, and we ate nothing but yams, fruit and berries. Roy's dysentery attacked him repeatedly, and with increasing frequency we had to stop until his cramping pain eased off.

Don fell into a morose, unsociable silence. Skinny grumbled plaintively and rarely treated us to his flashes of humour. Roy was too weak to care about anything. Just keeping alive was for him as much as he could manage. There was a sort of power, outside our own volition, that drove us on and on, and we developed a kind of tolerance of each other, so that, despite our uninhibited language, there was never a quarrel between us. If bad feeling had arisen it would have come from Skinny; but there were two of us, Don and I, who refused to let him taunt the party into any sort of unpleasantness.

Once, as we had just broken camp, there was a confused flurry on the track in front of me, and I cracked my stave down on a krait. When I held the stick up, the thin snake, like a black and gold thong, was coiled round it. It had a tiny bullet head, and it was quite dead.

On the twelfth day, suddenly and unexpectedly, we came to a river—a wide stretch of water, motionless and darkly green. We sat and looked at it.

"Why not float a raft down it?" said Roy.

"Down where?"

"To the coast."

"Some hope," said Skinny. "Look at the water."

It was hardly moving. We threw in a couple of branches, and they lay almost motionless. It was ten minutes before they had drifted out of sight. We made our way along the bank for half a mile, looking for a point of crossing, but there was none.

"Looks like a swim," I said.

"What about crocs?"

"One of us must go first and find out."

"Count me out," grunted Skinny.

Don looked him up and down. "We're all in this and you'll take your chance with the rest of us."

He pulled out an old mildewed coin and we tossed for the doubtful honour of first across.

125

Don lost.

Fully dressed, he slid into the deep, green water and without fuss or hesitation swam across in an easy Australian crawl. It struck me that for a man who was supposed to be past his prime and was certainly weak from lack of food, he set all of us a fine example. At last, on the other bank, he waded out, spluttering lime from his mouth and pulling the weeds that had twined themselves round his legs. He gave the thumbs-up sign, and together the rest of us entered the water and with much splashing started to swim towards the far bank. Roy panted all the way and Skinny jerked himself along in a fantastic cascade of water, half butterfly, half breast stroke. With nearly every breath we took we swallowed the yellow, sickly slime. But at last we reached the southern shore.

For another day we followed the track, now heading south-south-west. Late on the thirteenth afternoon there came, in the damp, humid air, the tang of burning sandalwood. We stopped. Then carefully we pushed forward until at last we spotted through the trees the tops of a cluster of atap huts. Easing cautiously forward, we caught sight of five or six natives, dressed only in loincloths. I was scared that there might be Japanese about, so we lay hidden in the jungle, some ten or fifteen yards apart, and watched the kampong. Soon a group of native women came towards us, but they turned along a path to a wooden trough from which they drew water. Near the trough we noticed a pile of what seemed to be edible roots and yams.

"Women!" whispered Skinny.

"Wrap up, Romeo," snapped Don.

We remained hidden outside the kampong until well after dark, then in the faint light from the stars we edged towards the water trough. It was pure rainwater, sweet and cool, and like animals at a desert oasis, we gulped it down, lifting our heads whenever we heard a sound, our hair dripping over our eyes. Only some fifteen yards away a handful of natives were clustered round a fire and we could smell food cooking. They neither saw nor heard us. Stealthily we crossed to the pile of roots; each of us grabbed a handful and made off with our prize to the trail on the other side of the village. There we climbed into the low, broad branches of a tree and sat gnawing for a long time at the sweet, crisp flesh of the yams.

We could hardly bear to leave the village; we longed for the nearness of fellow men; but we decided for safety's sake to push on some two miles before lying up for the night.

It was early the next day that Roy started to crack up. Early in the afternoon he stumbled and fell face downwards on the cool, spongy earth.

"I can't go on, Mac," he whispered. "I just can't."

We crowded round him. "This tree-sleeping's not doing us any good," grunted Don—we had for the last fortnight been spending each night wedged into the forks of some convenient tree—"we're not getting enough sleep. Let's try and find a spot clear of ants and camp there two or three days."

We agreed, and just off the trail found a patch of open ground which we dug with our staves until we were sure there were no ants. We covered it with ferns and broad, fleshy leaves from the undergrowth and lay down. We slept for a few hours, then at dusk roused up; Don, Skinny and I scouted around for food. We found a fair number of wild pineapples which quenched our thirst well enough, though some odd, acid content in their pulp made the sides of our mouths sore. We returned to our shelter and slept soundly through the night.

Next morning we were much refreshed, though Roy was weak and ill. About noon we scouted round the little clearing. Not far away we found ourselves out of the jungle and facing a road—a black ribbon of bitumen winding through the trees, wide enough to thin the laced foliage overhead and let through a filter of light. We dodged back into the undergrowth and lay for several hours watching the road. Some ox carts passed along, led by natives in loincloths, and then just before dark came a convoy of half a dozen battered lorries driven by Chinese.

We stayed close to the road for three days, feeding off fruit and drinking from a little spring which we found seeping in rivulets through a mound of rocks. Gradually we regained our strength. Then on the third day there came the whine of a distant car engine and a very neat Army staff car whistled past us; in it were six Japanese.

The sight of those Japs—the first we had seen for over three weeks—altered all our plans. We gathered as much fruit as we could, took a last refreshing drink from the spring, and decided again to head for the mountains, towering in a purple haze along the western horizon.

Day after day we plodded on. Each morning the mountains seemed a little nearer, and the nights became a little colder. The lush tropical jungle slowly gave way to short, spiky grass, trailing brambles and thorn-like shrubs which scratched and tore at our legs; the slight wounds festered and developed into running sores. Day after day there was no water to be found and none of the thirst-quenching fruits. Hunger and thirst hit us again, and soon our need for water grew desperate. But still we headed on and on over the undulating foothills.

We were without water for three days and four nights, until—for the second time since leaving Pasir Panjang—we faced the stark prospect of dying of thirst. Our tongues were swollen and leathery in our dried-up mouths, and each of us had occasional spells of dizziness. Unless we drank something we would die. It was not, I decided, a time to be squeamish. With the stem of a creeper I tied together one of the legs of my shorts. The others watched me. I filled the leg with handfuls of earth. Then I urinated into it. Underneath I held the dried gourd of a durian and watched the liquid slowly filtering through. The others stared at me with fascinated intensity. I took a little into my mouth and swallowed, crinkling up my face in revulsion and disgust.

"It's bitter," I said. But I drank it down.

"I'm game," said Skinny. He followed my example, and so did the others.

Afterwards we retched once or twice. But it seemed to have helped.

At any rate we slept.

But late that night I heard Roy moaning softly in his sleep. "Water," he whispered brokenly. "Water, for God's sake' water." His fingers curled and uncurled on the short, parched-up grass.

Chapter Six

The next morning I woke early. The sun, climbing into a sky of metallic blue, hung like a burning glass above an arid world of stone outcrops and undulating grassland. Soon the others were awake too, and for all of us thirst was no longer a discomfort but a torture. Either we found water or within forty-eight hours we should die. Don favoured trying to retrace our steps to the jungle kampong; but that called for a four-day march, and I doubted if we had the strength. I looked across at Roy. He was propped against a tree trunk, his face blue-white and haggard, his cheeks sunken, his eyes staring and the size of half-pennies. I wondered if he was dying.

I remembered that a tiny rivulet had come slanting in from the west, and on the fringe of the jungle had crossed diagonally over the tarmac road; if only we could hit the rivulet further upstream, among the foothills. I stared at the rounded, dark-blue mountains now less than fifty miles away; at one point the V-shaped shadow of a valley stood out blackly against the shaded blue. Could it be the valley of our rivulet? To head towards it seemed our only chance. And so we set off slowly, at right angles to our original course, into the barren foothills. Soon the scrubs gave way to rocks, stone outcrops and little precipitous cliffs some twenty to fifty feet high and topped with coarse yellow grass.

It was about midday that we heard a sharp, hollow bark. We stood motionless, then, as the bark echoed again, slipped behind a large boulder. After a while, Don eased himself forward, his eyes searching the rock face above our heads. We heard him gasp.

"Looks like a family of orang-utans," he said. Cautiously we stepped out of our hiding place and peered up to where he was pointing. There, less than fifty yards away, were three large orang-utans staring down at us.

"Take it easy, Don," I whispered. "There might be a whole tribe of them. We shouldn't stand much chance if they go for us."

For nearly a quarter of an hour we stood staring each other out—the four men and the three animals. Two of them were huge fellows, nearly six feet high; the other half their size.

"Daddy, Mummy and Little Lord Fauntleroy," whispered Skinny hoarsely, and even as he spoke the three animals turned and scrambled up a shallow scree, the biggest of them coming back for a last quizzical glance at us from behind a rock.

"We should have asked them where the nearest pub was," cackled Skinny.

We made a wide detour round the scree up which the orang-utans had disappeared.

That afternoon, with less shade from the sun, our walking slowed down to a heavy-footed lope, and eventually Roy became too weak to carry on. Skinny propped him up in the shade of the rock face and stayed with him, while Don and I started foraging for food.

Searching, not very optimistically, I came across a rotting tree trunk. Trying to reach a cluster of bitter-looking berries that grew across it, I stepped onto the log; but my foot slipped and the soft, mouldering wood broke away, revealing a colony of tiny tree bugs, pasty white in colour and crawling agitatedly over each other in their panic to find shelter.

"Skinny," I yelled. "Come here quickly."

I heard him jump up and come pounding over the loose stones.

"Off with your singlet, man," I said. "We've got food."

"What! Where?"

"Don't argue. Just take it off."

He looked at me as if I were crazy, then, thinking perhaps that he'd better humour me, he stripped off his sweat-soaked singlet and passed it over.

Don, hearing my call, came across. "Give me a hand," I said.

Between us we scooped up handfuls of the white, wriggling bugs, sloping them into the singlet until we had a fair-sized pile of quivering organic matter. Then I tied the ends of the singlet together and smashed it about a dozen times against a rock until there appeared through the grey cloth a pale pink stain. When I opened the singlet up there was inside, a sort of reddish jelly.

"The Sakais in Malaya taught me this," I said. "If they can stand it, so can we."

And taking some of the jelly between my fingers I forced myself to eat it. Don and Skinny looked at each other apprehensively; but we were all far too famished to be squeamish, and after a little they both took and ate a handful of the jelly, which had the furry texture of rhubarb, without the acid taste. We ate three-quarters of it, taking the last quarter back to Roy. He was dozing, almost in a coma, but we roused him up and forced some of the mixture between his swollen lips. He could scarcely swallow it.

"Wake up, Roy," I urged him. "Here's some fruit for you."

His heavy eyelids lifted and he looked at me blankly; at last his lips parted and I pushed a little of the mixture on to his white-coated tongue. As he opened his mouth I saw the web of sticky mucus stretching like transparent rubber from his tongue to the roof of his mouth. After much coaxing he finished his share of the food.

That pulp was all we had to eat for the rest of the day—apart from a few bitter berries, which were woody and dry, with no moisture in them. That night our thirst was worse—much worse—and we slept hardly at all. As soon as dawn broke we moved off, again through the rocky, waterless hills. Progress was slow, for all of us were feeling weak and dizzy. We took turns to help Roy along by holding his arms, one on either side of him. Late in the morning we found three flying foxes which seemed to have struck the rocks in flight, and lay dead on the arid hillside. Taking two that were untouched by ants or maggots, we tugged the skins off their bodies and forced ourselves to eat the raw flesh.

By the afternoon we were again moving with painful slowness. I was thinking of calling another halt, when Don suddenly lurched towards an outcrop of rock, fell on his knees and grabbed at something which was scuttling along the ground. Grinning broadly he stood up, in his hand a writhing green frog, some nine inches long. We skinned it, and passed round the few slivers of off-white flesh, swallowed them raw. But solid food, even in such minute quantities, was more than we could keep down, and half an hour later we vomited it up. That evening we all felt our strength ebbing inexorably away.

Then, quite suddenly, we saw ahead of us the ribbon of tarmac road, and running beside it a thin belt of vegetation. Where there was vegetation there would surely be water too. As though in a dream we saw the thin, clear trickle of water cascading down between dark, mossy boulders. Once again, at the last moment we had been saved from certain death.

For a long, long time we lay flat on our stomachs gulping down the cooling water and holding our heads under the fast-flowing current so that water trickled through our hair and down our necks. Under its cooling power I felt as through I were being born again, life flooding back into every tissue of my body.

For three days and nights we camped in a small green clearing screened by thick and heavy leaves. We fed mainly on fern roots and young bamboo shoots that, for all their earthy taste, were nourishing enough. We also found some wild pineapple, acid but juicy. And from the stream we drank and drank and drank. Our swollen tongues gradually contracted and our mouths were no longer sore and dry. Roy was the only one who did not completely recover, though even he rallied a little and lost for the time being that gaunt, deathly pallor that had frightened us so much.

We were at first afraid to leave our heaven-sent oasis, but gradually we accepted the fact that we could not stay for ever, and on the fourth day we decided to move on. We stuffed as many pineapple and fern roots as possible into our shorts, which we tied round our necks, wrapping strips from our shirts round our loins native fashion. We all had scabby sores on our legs where we had been scratched by the thorn-like bushes and the lalang grass, and the open wounds had festered and then dried in the sun. Also the scars on my face had opened up, for the sword-cuts from the Japanese officer had never healed properly.

The last night we spent in the clearing it began to rain. It was a soft but drenching rain that continued until the early morning, when the sky cleared and the moon filtered her pale light through the rain-spangled leaves. The clearing lay in silence, bathed in ethereal light that silvered and refined the lust, exotic undergrowth. It was so light that we decided it would be better, until the moon waned, to journey by night and sleep by day. It would be cooler that way and there would be less chance of our meeting Japanese—for we had decided to follow the road and river as long as they headed south-westward together. Our last day in the clearing we enjoyed an unbroken sleep of more than eight hours. Then at dusk we moved off again, heading roughly south-south-west—a course which if we followed it would take us diagonally across the island, over the southern extremity of the mountains.

We took things easily that first night, covering only about six miles, because Roy was still shaky. We found a lot of the prickly-pear berry and used up none of the food supply we carried with us. The next day we slept a few yards off the road hidden in the undergrowth, and at dusk started walking again. At dawn the following morning we were searching for a suitable spot to camp down, when we came to a clump of coconut palms in what must have once been a cultivated patch but was now thickly covered with undergrowth. I saw the palms first, and shinned up one of the trees and knocked down a dozen or so of the nuts, Don smashed them against the trunk until they split. They were green and soft but the milk in them was rich and sweet. We kept several back, ready for our journey that night, then, hidden again in the undergrowth, we dozed off to sleep.

We followed the road for seven nights, and in the early hours of the eighth came to a burned-out shed. The charred timbers were still standing, surrounded by a grey-white carpet of ashes, and not far away were the bodies of two Chinese; the telltale marks of the bayonet were all too obvious.

"Jap handiwork," grunted Don.

The rest of us did not speak but stood staring at the mutilated bodies.

"Let's get out of this," muttered Skinny.

As we turned to leave, I noticed another body—this time that of a child, so lacerated it was impossible to tell the sex. As I kicked over the charred wood and ashes I came across a tin mug and a rusty old knife. I picked them up, and Skinny looked at me with obvious disgust.

"Live and let live," I said. "They won't want them now." And, with more than usual caution, we moved on.

Just before sunrise the road narrowed, and in the grey half-light we saw ahead the outline of a kampong. We hid just off the road in a sprawling clump of bushes, watching and waiting until, as the sun rose, we could make out the dark outlines of some sixty huts, each on its raised stilts.

"Another lakeside village," I whispered to Don. "Quite a biggish one, about five hundred people I'd say."

The first to begin work were the women, and we watched them carrying water in large earthen jars from a nearby stream. Then they lit fires and we caught the succulent smell of cooking fish. Our mouths began to water.

"Shall we go in?" whispered Don.

"What if there are Japs about?" I muttered. "It would be plain suicide. Anyway, the natives mayn't be friendly."

Don looked across at Roy, whose lips were cracked and swollen and who was again nearly doubled up with dysentery.

"What about him?"

"We'll have to hold on," I answered. "It would be mad to walk in, in broad daylight."

All day we lay hidden; through the long morning and the hot, steamy afternoon when the rain again pattered down on the leaves over our heads. Towards evening Roy began to mutter to himself in half-delirium. A little before sunset I turned to Don.

"I'm going in," I said. "If I'm not back within the hour, you three clear out."

I crawled through the bushes to the edge of the kampong, then stood up, my nerves tingling. I was ready to run for it at the slightest sign of hostility, but tried to look unconcerned as I walked across the hard-trodden earth, passing two elderly natives in loincloths who showed not the slightest interest in me. I walked through the centre of the village, past a doorless building from which I could smell the tantalizing aroma of coffee, until the huts began to thin out. I realized the natives were stopping to stare at me and turned backed on my tracks, back to the hut where I had smelt the coffee. I decided to make a bold approach. I went up to the doorway and stood there motionless so they could study me; and I could study them.

It must have been a village coffeeshop, for inside were a small group of Indonesians sitting at a rough bamboo table, and on a wooden counter a kerosene tin of coffee bubbled over a small flame.

Behind the counter stood a fat, expressionless Chinese in a loose, threadbare smock. The Indonesians sat quite still, staring at me without expression. I went up to the Chinese, and spoke softly.

"Mana Jippon?"

He stared at me for a full minute, then replied in Malay, "No Japanese here."

"I have no food. May I eat?"

"Where are you from"

I pointed vaguely to the north.

"There are others with you?"

"Yes, three others. One is sick."

He looked at me hard. "Wait," he said, and went out of the door.

My hand slid down to the parang which was tied around my waist. I edged towards the door and waited close to one of the Indonesians. If there were trouble, I should use him as a shield.

In a few minutes the Chinese returned; with him was an old man with a wizened face and a fringe of white hair. Dangling from a silver chain round his neck was a medal which, as he stepped towards me, I recognized as the Queen Wilhelmina medal for faithful service.

"Selamat," I said.

"Selamat," he answered, peering at me keenly as though he were short-sighted. "Where do you come from?"

Again I pointed to the north.

"Have you come far?"

"Yes, very far."

"What are you doing here? All the white men left many weeks ago."

"Where did they go to?" I countered.

"I do not know. But why are you not with your own people?"

"We had to remain behind. Then the Japanese came and we were captured, but later we escaped."

"You are not of the Company?"

"The Company?" I repeated, not understanding.

"Yes, are you a member of the Company?"

Then I realized what he meant. In many remote districts of Java and Sumatra the Dutch Government was known as the Company.

"No," I answered, "I am not."

"You are English?"

"Yes."

"From Singapore perhaps?"

"Yes."

"Soldiers? Fighting the Japanese?"

"Yes."

"That is good, very good."

"Are there any Japanese here?"

"There are many soldiers ten miles away."

"How many, and whereabouts?"

"Perhaps seven or eight hundred. To the south and the west."

That puts paid to our plan of cutting diagonally across the island, I thought.

"Old man," I said, "my friend is very sick."

"Go and bring him, together with the others. We will care for you."

I walked out of the door, past the crowd of natives who had gathered on the threshold, and back into the jungle. Don, Skinny and

Roy were so well hidden that it took me some time to locate them, but finally I found the thicket where they were concealed.

"It's OK, Don," I said. "We can go in."

"Might be a trap?"

"I don't think so. Anyhow, we must have help for Roy."

"OK, cobber. You're the boss."

I told the others that as we were offered hospitality, we must untie our parangs and put them on one side; this was customary in a friend's house. Then we walked together into the kampong. Outside the coffeeshop the old man was waiting for us. He escorted us inside, into the now empty room, and we laid our parangs on the counter.

I pointed to Roy.

"He is very sick."

The old man went across to a younger native who was waiting outside the doorway and spoke rapidly to him. Then he turned to me. "He will bring medicine," he said.

After a few moments, another native came in and offered us each a bowl of liquid that tasted like distilled alcoholic curry. It flamed down our gullets and almost at once I felt energy returning. The old man was quietly watching us.

"What are the Japanese doing here?" I asked him.

"They are bad men, very bad men," he said. "All day and all night they eat and drink and kill anyone who passes. The first Japanese were good soldiers, but those that are left now are different. They drink and take away our women."

"If we travel south, can we pass through these Japanese?"

"Perhaps, if you are careful. But there is no more fighting here. There is fighting in Java, much fighting."

"Then we must get there."

"It would take many days; and how would you cross the water between Sumatra and Java?"

As he spoke, a woman entered the hut with a bowl containing a few handfuls of white powder. She stood waiting. The old man pointed to Roy, and she nodded. She crossed to him and in sign language motioned him to lie down and take off the rags round his loins.

"Crikey," said Skinny. "In broad daylight too!"

I told Roy that she wanted to treat him for his dysentery.

"Good God, Mac," he whispered. "I can't strip in front of a native woman." If his face had not been burned black by the sun, I would have sworn that he was blushing. But I persuaded him to do as she asked. He lay face downwards, naked below the waist, and the woman placed one hand under his stomach and raised him gently so that his back was arched. Then she poured a little of the white powder on to him and eased it in with her fingers.

"Enjoying yourself?" said Skinny.

The look on poor Roy's face made us explode with laughter.

"He will be better tomorrow," said the woman, and with a smile she left the hut. I thanked her.

"Where did you learn to speak my language?" the old man asked.

"In Malaya. I had many good friends among the Malays."

He turned to the Chinese, who had re-entered the hut together with a crowd of gaping natives. "Have you a cigarette for my friend?" he asked him.

From a battered packet the Chinese offered me one, which I

accepted. Then I remembered that according to Malay custom it is impolite to take a cigarette without offering it first to your host and that, for religious reasons, you should also accept it with the left hand. So I took the cigarette, a little clumsily, and offered it to the old man. He smiled broadly, showing his few isolated teeth.

"Thank you," he said.

He was still smiling when a native rushed breathlessly through the door, rolling his eyes toward us, and whispered urgently in the old man's ear. We were at once pushed out of the coffeeshop, led a few yards across a clearing and then into the doorway of another hut, through that and out of an opening at the back, down a short flight of rough steps and into a pile of decaying refuse.

"Hey, what goes on?" grunted Skinny.

"Shut up," I snapped at him. "I heard the old boy mutter 'Jippon'."

We peered out from the refuse dump through a rough wooden palisade.

"Blimey," muttered Don. "Japs."

Not thirty yards away, their figures indistinct in the gathering twilight, stood four Japanese privates with rifles slung round their backs, their peaked caps pulled by chin-straps low over their foreheads. Beyond them an officer was talking to the old man.

"Keep quiet, for God's sake," I muttered.

We lay there, hardly daring to breathe—which was just as well, for the smell from the rubbish was appalling.

We stayed there, hardly stirring, until it was quite dark. But at last we heard an engine starting up. Peering through the palisade we saw in the pale moonlight a truck disappearing out of the village, the four Jap soldiers huddled together in the back of it. A few minutes later the old man came over and beckoned us out of our hiding place. As he shepherded us across the clearing he explained that the Japanese had come to demand young men from the village for field labour.

"I said that all our young men had left the village, but they were persistent," he told me. "However, that is our worry. You can now forget the Japanese, and sleep."

We followed him up the steps of an atap hut; its floor was covered with rushes. We were given bowls of hot curry and as much water as we needed. That night we slept with full stomachs and with our spirits higher than they had been since, nearly a month ago, we had left the kampong at Medan. Shelter and the company of fellow men had made us realize we were still human beings.

By the time we woke next morning the sun had already risen high. By common impulse we looked over to where Roy was sleeping. He was breathing easily and there was for the first time in weeks a little colour to his cheeks. When he woke we asked how he was feeling.

"Don't know yet. It's a bit early." He stretched, smiling, yawned and rose carefully.

"H'm. Pretty good," he said. He was looking better than at any time since leaving Pasir Panjang.

"Reckon I'll ask for a pennyworth of your popsy," said Skinny.

After we had eaten a type of Malayan hotpot—basically curry mixed with fish, and very satisfying—the Chinese from the coffeeshop appeared, silhouetted against the strong sun striking in through the open door. Behind him was the old man and a young, refined and cultured-looking Chinese, dressed in a clean silk sarong and freshly ironed trousers; when he smiled I caught the flash of gold teeth. The old man introduced him to us as Nang Sen.

Nang Sen was friendly and spoke to us in perfect English. He told us, as the old man had done the day before, that the Japanese had been through the village some weeks ago and had raped many of the girls. Since then they had been back several times, demanding field labour.

"But what about you?" he asked. "Where are you aiming for?"

"We aim to keep clear of the Japs," I answered, "and try to join up with any of our troops who are still fighting."

He looked at me closely. "I shall be driving a lorry south in a few days' time, almost to the coast. You and your friends can come with me if you like; then try to cross to Java. There is still fighting there. You are English and so I will help you. If you were Dutch I would not."

"Why?" I asked him.

"We do not like the Dutch here. We hope that one day the English will come, drive out the Japanese and take Sumatra for themselves."

I looked at him curiously.

"For many years," he went on, "I have been fighting against the Japanese in China."

"And who are you fighting for now?" I asked. "Not for the Chinese still?"

He smiled, and made some trivial excuse to leave.

Later that morning an Indonesian woman came into our hut while we were dozing, huddled against the wooded walls. The fat Chinese was with her.

"We have water for you outside," he said. "Perhaps you would like to wash; then the women will clean your clothes."

We made our way to a little clearing behind one of the huts, stripped down, and splashed about in the buckets of water that we found waiting. The Chinese took away our filthy, tattered clothes, and left others for us after we had washed. Our bodies were burned the colour of Jacobean oak and, as we splashed about quite naked, the patches of skin round our loins where the sun had not touched looked like white shorts. How emaciated we all looked; but we returned to the hut, feeling like Tibetan monks in our long, flowing robes, and glowing all over with physical wellbeing. Another woman was waiting for us. She carried tiny bowls of a green herbal ointment which she rubbed with soft, gently fingers into the sores on our legs and on my face, cooling the festered flesh round open, unhealed wounds. So much human kindness, after weeks of loneliness and hardship, was strangely moving.

Curried rice, sweet boiled roots and green shoots were again provided for lunch. When we had eaten our fill we again dozed until the evening, when Nang Sen came to visit us. He seemed glad to have us to talk to, and until well after sundown the five of us sat on our haunches exchanging news and opinions. Java, he told us, had fallen in March and Sumatra in April; though in the latter island the Japanese were more or less confined to the coastal regions.

"There are parts of Sumatra," he said with a smile, "where the Japanese dare not go."

It was a somewhat different story, he told us, in Java, where most of the natives, duped by propaganda, had gone over to the Japanese without resistance; and apart from the southern corner of the island, where there was much guerrilla fighting, the Japs were everywhere firmly established. There had been an Englishman, he said, an Air

Force officer, who had been conducting a guerrilla war in Java, but he had been caught.

"Do you know his name?" I asked.

"No. He was a very large man, but that's all I can tell you. I know there are many British prisoners in Java; most of them from Malaya. Many ships were sunk in the Malacca Strait, and the troops who were not drowned are almost all prisoners."

"Do you know anything of a ship called the *Wakefield*?" I asked him quickly.

"Two ships, the *West Point* and the *Wakefield*, left Singapore almost together. One was sunk at once; nobody knows what happened to the other, but the Japanese say she was sunk later in the Indian Ocean."

"I suppose Australia is still free," grunted Don cynically.

"Oh yes," said Nang Sen, "for the time being. But the Japs talk of the day when they will capture Australia and New Zealand."

None of us laughed. After the slick ease with which they had taken Malaya, Java and Sumatra, we would have been surprised at nothing. Don leaned forward.

"Look," he said. "Tell us frankly, what are our chances of reaching Australia?"

"Not too good. You would need to be very tough and very lucky. Even if you got as far as Java, it would take months, perhaps years, to reach Australia."

But the fact that he reckoned our reaching Australia was not completely out of the question filled us with optimism.

For two days we stayed in the kampong, gradually becoming stronger and less tired. Our cheeks began to lose their hollows and

Roy no longer stared at us through dark, saucer-like eyes. The woman returned our clothes; they still retained the stains from ingrained sweat and grime, but at least they no longer stank. Our sores were healing quickly.

Early on the third morning Nang Sen mounted the steps in our hut.

"I'm leaving today for Palembang," he told us. "I expect you'd like to come?"

"You bet," said Don. "How are you travelling?"

"By lorry. There is room for the four of you. I'm taking rubber sheeting and you can hide under it."

Palembang we knew was on the coast, in the far south of Sumatra; another step on the way to Australia.

At about noon Nang Sen led us to a clearing on the edge of the kampong where a group of chattering natives were clustered round an ancient lorry; there was hardly a speck of paint on it.

"What is it?" I asked him.

"A Chrysler. I got it from the Japanese."

"From the Japs?"

"Yes. I told them I'd lost mine during the fighting. I knew they'd want me to collect rubber for them so I guessed they'd give me this. The Japanese think I'm a very good man; they think I am their friend and tell them everything. So I tell them everything, but only that part of everything which I want them to know." He laughed.

We piled into the back of the lorry and lay down while the villagers covered us with layer after layer of thick, raw rubber. It smelt appalling. The engine was cranked by hand then roared into life; Nang Sen smacked in his gear and we catapulted forward.

For the greater part of that day we travelled in the ancient, rattling vehicle, bumping over a rough jungle track. The heat under the rubber was at times more than we could stand without fainting, and almost every half-hour we had to push up the heavy sheets and gulp down lungfuls of fresh, cool air. Towards evening Nang Sen ran his lorry off the road behind a cluster of bushes in soft, damp ground that must have been on the fringe of a swamp. Here was another kampong; a handful of raised atap huts, and a few natives, wearing loincloths and coolie hats wandered aimlessly about. We pulled off our sweat-sodden clothes, and felt the cool, fresh air flow over our greasy skins. Nang Sen came across to us with three other Chinese, to whom we were smilingly introduced as friends.

"My people will look after you," he said. "I must go now, but I shall return shortly. I'm fetching petrol from a Japanese post two miles away. Do you wish to come too?"

"Not even to say thank you for the petrol."

He smiled, bowed formally, and climbed into the driver's seat. With a spluttering cough the Chrysler moved slowly off, rolling and bumping down the twilit jungle track.

"What do you make of Nang Sen?" I whispered, as the lorry disappeared.

"Queer fellow," Don muttered. "He's well in with the Japs. Suppose he's ratting on us, and now he's off to tell them where we are?"

"Not likely. He could have tipped them off at the kampong."

"Yes, I suppose he's OK."

As we stood talking, a man with the slit eyes and high cheekbones of a Chinese approached us.

"I should not worry, gentlemen," he said in perfect English. "Nang Sen is a very good man. We cannot yet beat the Japanese in open warfare, but all of us await the day when our people come; then we shall fight with them."

"The Chinese?" I asked.

"Yes. Soon Chiang Kai Shek will come, then we shall fight."

We walked towards an atap hut, outside which stood a trestle-table; on it we found bowls of rice. Don, Roy and Skinny started to eat hungrily, but I was intrigued by our Chinese host.

"And the people of Sumatra?" I prompted him. "Will they fight with you?"

"They do not really care who rules them. They think only of their day-to-day existence, and provided no one maltreats them, they are content. The Japanese have learned that lesson, and are trying to be friendly."

"But you aren't Chinese. You speak like an Englishman."

He laughed. "I am half Chinese, a quarter English, and a quarter Malay. A real Christmas pudding."

I glanced at his loose silk smock and ankle-length trousers, noting the lithe body underneath.

"Anything less like a Christmas pudding," I said, "I've never met."

Donaldson put his rice bowl aside and joined the conversation.

"If we get to Java," he asked, "what are our chances?"

"I am not sure about the southern part. In the north, of course, you'll be all right; we shall tell them about you."

"Tell them? About us?"

"Yes. We have friends there."

Don pulled thoughtfully at his beard. "Who exactly are you fighting for?"

The young man looked at him closely. "For the independence of the New East Indies," he replied.

It was very late when Nang Sen returned; he suggested we stayed the next day in the kampong to recover from the journey; there was, he told us, a wedding in the village, and we could join in the celebrations. This suited us admirably, as we were all tired and bruised from our five hours' hiding in the lorry. Before we dozed off, we discussed our reception in the kampong. Don was in favour of moving off on our own, for he distrusted Nang Sen and feared that we should find ourselves involved in some political intrigue. But Skinny said that he had been talking to an old Chinese in the kampong and that, though neither could interpret the other's language very well (which, knowing Skinny's Indonesian, we could readily understand), he had gathered that another European—an Army major—had visited the village only a few weeks ago before and had been helped by Nang Sen.

"Did you get his name?" asked Don.

"No, only his rank," said Skinny. We decided to risk staying on, and soon dropped off to sleep.

Next morning we watched the village wedding. Both Chinese and Indonesians were dressed in their best raiment; no work was done, but as soon as the sum had risen, and while it still cast long shadows from the raised huts and the tall trees that encircled the kampong, the bride and bridegroom were escorted to the clearing in the centre of the village. Two high-backed bamboo chairs were in position, one for the bride and the other from the groom. The girl could not have been more than fourteen or fifteen, but her young breasts showed firm beneath her bead-embroidered baju. Throughout the morning and early afternoon she sat there, silent, with her head downcast, looking demurely at the ground, while the young man in his chair beside her, a garland of flowers round his neck, chatted with and received presents from the villagers, like a king holding audience. The sun rose to its zenith, then slid slowly behind the tall trees into a bank of low cloud. Silently now, the villagers gathered round the young couple, completely circling them. Don, Skinny, Roy and I were squatting on our haunches watching. Fires had been lit around the clearing, and as the dancing flames threw fantastic, twisting shadows over the waiting people, the bridegroom rose to his feet. He turned to the quiet girl beside him and gently raised her by the arms, smiling down at her and lifting her head so that their eyes met and she smiled back at him. Then he loosened his sarong and wrapped it round her so that its wide folds encompassed them both. Under its cover she dropped her own sarong and together they stepped over it towards the hut that had been prepared for them, gaily decorated with festoons of flowers.

The departure of the couple was the signal for merrymaking. Feasting and dancing started and continued long into the night, and together with the villagers we drank a potent, burning liquid of syrup-like smoothness until all of us were heady and sleepy. Late in the evening rain poured down from a leaden sky, but the fires continued to burn brightly and there was no let-up to the rejoicing. The groom and his bride were left to themselves, untroubled by the excited, sometimes frenzied, villagers.

We rose late next morning and drank several pints of water to relieve our legacy of thirst from the brew we had drunk the night before. Each of us had a first-class hangover, but Nang Sen, seemingly unaffected by the celebrations, visited us soon after breakfast and said he wanted to move on as soon as possible.

So we made our farewells—there was no sign of the newly married couple—and took our places once more in the back of the lorry. Soon we were again gasping and sweating under the thick rubber sheets, and breathing the fumes from the cans of petrol and paraffin that were stowed all around us. It was evening before we made our first stop. Then Nang Sen pulled away the sheets of rubber and produced some fruit and dried fish wrapped in thick, sappy leaves; as we ate he told us we would have to travel by night because Jap patrols were known to be in the area. They did not, he said, like operating at night.

The sky was black and starless that night as Nang Sen drove on, hour after hour. Sometimes we followed a made-up road; sometimes we bumped over jungle tracks, crisscrossed by tree roots as thick as the coils of an octopus. This time we lay on top of the cargo of rubber and, if we were bounced about as though tossed on a sprung mattress, at least we were more comfortable and could breathe. Nang Sen certainly knew his way, for he did not stop again until a little before dawn when we ran off the track into dense undergrowth.

The ground under our feet squelched alarmingly as we jumped from the lorry, and I at once noticed the swarms of mosquitoes buzzing round our legs.

"Much malaria here," Nang Sen told us. He led the way to what looked like a cinchona bush—about the size of a rhododendron—and snapped off a handful of the dark, shiny leaves.

"Chew these," he said. "They have quinine in them."

They tasted almost unbearable bitter, but Nang Sen told us to go on chewing until there was no more sap. He stood amused, watching our grimaces, and afterwards offered us some betel nuts wrapped in leaves; these we crunched until the bitter taste had disappeared.

Before we settled down to sleep in a shaded patch of lush grass under a cluster of low-branched bushes that offered protection from the sun but not from the mosquitoes, Nang Sen pointed to a stunted jungle palm whose fern-like leaves spread outwards like a fan. He jabbed a knife into the soft, pulpy trunk and out gushed a pale greenish liquid which he drank.

"Try it," he said.

We all drank, somewhat gingerly at first. The liquid was slightly sour, but not unpleasant.

"Water," said Nang Sen. "Where the palm grows, man need never die of thirst."

We slept through the hot day and travelled again at night; and the next day followed the same procedure. As dawn broke on the third morning, we ran into a populated area, passing groups of native huts and a few burned-out European houses. Nang Sen slowed down and finally drove the lorry into a wide, shallow defile just off the road. We clambered out and he led us through a plantation of rubber trees. He seemed to know exactly where he was, and after half an hour's brisk walking, led us into a kampong and over to one of the huts. He told us to wait, disappeared inside and almost at once came out again with a small, bird-like woman whom he introduced as his sister. She looked us over, then, in a flood of mixed Malay and Chinese, broke into a string of curses and complaints at our dishevelled appearance. We felt like naughty schoolchildren. She produced a selection of short smocks and thin cotton trousers of Chinese pattern. Then she rushed us firmly to a rain tub. "Wash," she said. "And properly."

"Any hope of a razor?" I asked.

Nang Sen produced one, but before I could begin to hack away with it, his sister appeared with a pair of scissors and snipped off the bulk of my beard, leaving me to use the razor on the last half-inch. The others also clipped their beards but preferred not to shave.

For two days we rested with Nang Sen and his sister, sleeping in rope beds and savouring the smell of incense which burnt from joss sticks placed near a little Buddha in a corner of our hut. In the evening of the second day Nang Sen came to bid us farewell. We were not, he told us, to worry, for his sister would care for us. But we must do exactly as she ordered, for we were now on the outskirts of Palembang and the Japanese were all around. His sister, whose name he pronounced like "Bow", would, he said, arrange for us to continue our journey south. He shook each of us warmly by the hand. I tried to thank him, but he would have none of it; he flashed his gold-toothed smile, turned on his heel and without a backward glance walked purposefully away. His going left us with a strange isolated feeling, as if we had lost one of our own company. We tried to question his sister when, about ten o'clock that night, she brought some hot curried rice, but her Malay was very limited, and coherent conversation was almost an impossibility.

An hour before dawn she roused us and told us to follow her. Surprised at the early start, we got up, shivering in the misty darkness, and, hardly awake, trekked after her slim figure through the rubber trees; we came soon to a rough track and followed it down until we caught the dank smell of water. Just as the sun was rising through a haze of pale golden mist, we came to a river. A little sampan, with a small square-rigged sail, was hidden in a shallow backwater. We climbed into it, pushed off, and "Bow" told the other three to lie down while I helped her paddle into midstream. Almost at once we rounded a bend in the river, and through the golden curtain of mist I could pick out the silhouette of several tall buildings overtopping a belt of atap huts on bamboo stilts.

"Palembang?" I asked.

She nodded.

We slid past the skeletons of bombed and burned-out wrecks nosing forlornly out of the water, and on one of the hulks I read the name "Perak"—a Straits boat. "Bow" steered the sampan to the opposite side of the river; the boat nosed into a soft bank of mud and we climbed ashore. We followed our guide in silence through a belt of secondary jungle to a small railway siding. Here she took us to a goods train consisting of a Heath Robinson-like engine and some fifteen or eighteen low trucks covered with tarpaulins. By one of these she halted and gestured us to climb in. This we did, and she tugged at the heavy rubber covering until we were well hidden.

"Friends will come soon," she whispered.

We heard, for a few seconds, the soft thread of her footsteps on the gravel; then she was gone.

We lay there for over an hour; soon we began to sweat as the sun filtered through the mist and brought heat to our cramped, airless hideout.

"I've had about enough of this," Don grumbled.

We were on the point of raising the tarpaulin and risking a look round when we heard an excited jabbering of voices along the track, topped by a harsh guttural staccato: obviously Japanese. To our horror the voices grew louder. Footsteps grated on the loose gravel and came to a halt beside the truck. We lay motionless, holding our breath. Suddenly bare feet thudded again the truck and with grunts and curses men came tumbling over the side and, above the tarpaulin, piled up on top of us. There was an excited jabbering in Indonesian, but, thank God, no staccato Japanese. The bodies above us jerked this way and that as the truck with a clanging rattle of wood and metal began to move slowly down the line.

We were half-suffocated; we felt as if our sides were cracking; but we dared not move. After some thirty minutes I could stand neither the physical strain nor the mental agony of not knowing who our companions were. Very carefully I eased back a corner of the tarpaulin. Immediately the daylight was blotted out, and a voice whispered, in soft Javanese, "Wait." I eased back again. Javanese!

A few minutes later there came a faint scratching at the tarpaulin, then the covering was rolled back and we were exposed, blinking stupidly in the strong sunlight. About a dozen Javanese were grinning down at us.

As we eased the blood back into our cramped limbs, the natives asked us to share some of their rice cakes packed in leaves, and they also offered us loosely rolled cigarettes. We squatted huddled together in the jolting truck, and I tried to question them. Had they known we were in the truck, I asked them. And where were we bound for? But conversation wasn't easy, for their language was unfamiliar to me, and we could only compromise on a form of bastard Malay.

"Did you know we were in the truck?"

"Yes."

"How did you know?"

"We were told."

"Who told you?"

The native shrugged his shoulders; "It isn't wise to ask."

After that conversation lapsed as the train jolted through kampongs, jungle and an occasional plantation. There were seventeen of us, packed tightly together in the small, dilapidated truck.

"Damned fine form of travel," grumbled Skinny. "Why couldn't we have a first-class carriage to ourselves?"

"Wrap up," grunted Don. "You're lucky to be travelling at all."

I noticed that Roy was looking sick again. How much longer, I wondered, could he stand the constant jolting? I spoke to another of the Javanese.

"Where are we going to?" I asked him.

"Oasthaven."

Oasthaven, I knew, was on the southern tip of Sumatra. "Are they many Japanese there?"

"Yes. Many."

"Will you help us hide from them?"

He shrugged his shoulders. Hour followed hour in the scorching truck. Roy was holding his hands flat on his stomach in spasmodic pain.

"I can't stand much more of this," he gasped after a specially vicious lurch.

"OK," I said. "I'll find out just where we are." I turned to the Javanese and asked him.

"In a few minutes," he said, "we come to Oasthaven."

"Will the train stop before we get there."

Again he shrugged his shoulders. I turned to Don.

"I don't like this," I muttered. "Reckon we'd better clear out."

"What about Nang Sen and his friends? Weren't they going to help us?"

"Maybe they've left us to fend for ourselves now."

It was early evening, and in the gathering gloom we could see the outlines of scattered huts, increasing in number, with a few stone buildings here and there. The train was slowing down. It was now or never.

"Let's go," I said.

The Javanese looked on, completely unperturbed, as, one after another, we slid over the side of the truck and dropped to the track. Roy went first and when I landed I ran back to where he was picking himself up; he was bent double in pain as he tried to struggle to his feet.

"OK, Roy?" I asked him.

"Yes Mac, thanks, I'm OK; but, by God, I'm glad to be out of that truck."

Together we made our way into the thick, long grass and bushes of secondary jungle that edged the railtrack. After a few minutes we came to a little patch of short grass under a spreading, low-branched tree; here we lay down and, when we had regained breath, discussed our plan of campaign. We decided to stay where we were overnight and I agreed to make a survey of Oasthaven the next morning.

Before it became quite dark we scouted round and unearthed the usual breadfruit, bamboo shoots and durian which had for the last six weeks formed our staple diet. Water we tapped from a palm tree in the way shown us by Nang Sen; but strangely enough, the only one who felt at all thirsty was Roy.

After the last vestige of daylight had drained from the tropical sky we became plagued by mosquitoes. Sleep did not come easily, and in the humid atmosphere we tossed and turned in fever-conscious restlessness. That night proved to be the prelude to a month of helpless suffering, beside which the hardships we had hitherto endured paled into insignificance.

Chapter Seven

In the early hours of the morning I awoke drenched in sweat and shivering, and I knew that neither that day nor for many days to come would I be walking the streets of Oasthaven. Malaria I had known before, but never an attack like this. My stomach was taut with almost incessant vomiting. My eyes throbbed hotly to an ever-changing pulse-beat, and my spine was cold as through packed in splintered ice. For three days I was scarcely conscious. I remember realizing that Don too was ill, and Roy so weak that he could hardly move. I remember Skinny padding worriedly about, sometimes trying to force water between my obstinately clenched teeth, sometimes trying to cover me with broad fern leaves against the rain that, hour after hour, filtered through the branches overhead.

On the fourth day, quite suddenly, the fever died away.

Skinny propped me up against the base of a tree and told me what had happened. I had, he said, been delirious; for hours at a stretch I had raved about Pat and our daughter and the *Wakefield*. He had thought I was dying. Don had been ill too—though his attack was not as bad as mine. Roy's dysentery was, at one point, so bad that Skinny had thought that he too would surely die. Now that both of us seemed to be recovering his relief was unbounded.

During the next couple of days Don and I managed to get on our feet a little and to walk slowly round the clearing, while Skinny was nurse, cook and breadwinner. Gradually our strength returned, and after another week had passed I suggested we again move on. Roy was still pitifully weak, but said he would keep up as best he could.

We decided to skirt round Oasthaven and make for the south-eastern tip of the island, which I calculated could not be too far distant. After much casting around we found a track running in a southerly direction. This we followed. Water was plentiful, as we crossed over a series of small trickling streams. We found plenty of coconuts too. Skinny, by now a seasoned trouper, shinned expertly up the trees and sent the nuts crashing down to us; the pulpy flesh was nourishing food and the sweet juice a refreshing drink. We halted early that evening, and when Skinny had gone off to forage for our meal, Don and I started to make Roy comfortable for the night. Presently Skinny returned, his arms laden with a number of small greenish fruits, not unlike the prickly pear. I tried one, and found it slightly bitter, but not at all unpleasant. Each of us ate several of the fruits, which seemed to satisfy both hunger and thirst. Then we settled down for the night. But sleep refused to come; each of us twisted restlessly to and fro, and gradually I became aware of an acute sexual embarrassment. I looked at the others. They too, it seemed, had a similar sensation. We sat up and looked at one another. It was so funny that I burst out laughing; but even laughter—usually so effective an antidote—brought no cure. The embarrassment lasted for nearly an hour before suddenly subsiding.

"Must have been the fruit," grunted Don, and rolling over he fell asleep.

But Skinny went on jabbering into the small hours; he would, he said, make his fortune after the war if only he could get the fruit back to be analysed. But at last he too fell asleep.

Next morning we pushed on again into a country of open scrub, the path winding through tangled undergrowth some three feet high. Day after day we walked on, stripped to the waist, the sun burning our bodies a deep mahogany. We met no living creature, neither man or beast.

"Reckon we'd pass for natives now," Don grunted once.

"Not me, cobber," I told him. "I've got blue eyes."

"We could pass as Eurasians though."

"Maybe."

We made slow progress as Roy was still weak, and every few minutes we had to stop and rest. Food was hard to come by, but water presented no problem as there were occasional streams, and scattered among the low scrub were a number of the palms Nang Sen had shown us, and by jabbing our knives into the bark, we tapped the sour, thin liquid. It was enough to slake our thirst. Gradually the berries, fruit and roots became scarcer, and, once again, hunger became something more than a discomfort.

Early one morning Skinny suddenly made a dash into the long grass and dived headlong into a shallow ditch. He rose triumphantly, in his hands a baby monkey; it was squeaking and clawing furiously. We killed it with a parang. Feeling a bit squeamish, we lit a fire, packed the monkey's body in mud and let it slowly roast in the ashes. When I took it out, the skin rolled easily away and we tore hungrily at the flesh with our fingers. It tasted sweet, but after a few mouthfuls Don threw his portion away, his face puckered in disgust.

"This is sheer cannibalism," he grunted.

Looking at what was left of the monkey, we felt sick, and somehow ashamed. I covered the body with a thick layer of earth and we again moved on.

That evening, as dusk began to drain the colour from our world of scrub and grassland and the sky became opaquely grey, we saw through the short trees a vague shimmering of water. It was not a river nor a lake. It was the sea: the south-eastern shore of Sumatra— eight hundred miles from the mangroves and mudflats of Medan.

Little wavelets were breaking on a shelving beach, breaking on to sand white as on the beaches of Brittany. But this beach was lined not with Breton cliffs but with stunted palms, and in the sheltered horseshoe of a little bay nestled a native kampong.

Since our most pressing need was medical care for Roy, we decided on a bold approach, and strode openly into the kampong, regardless of what our reception might be, or whether there were Japs about. At first the natives in their loincloths and coolie hats drew back timidly as we approached; then they clustered together in groups, muttering apprehensively—as well they might, for we must have been a fearsome-looking quartet.

Eventually the headman came to meet us. Like the leaders of the other kampongs, he was small, his face was wizened and he wore the Queen Wilhelmina medal. He scrutinized us keenly, but his prune-like face showed no sign of surprise. I approached him courteously. "Greetings, tuan," I said, hoping to impress him with my respect for his rank and age.

"Who are you?" he asked. "Where are you from?"

I told him we were Eurasian labourers trying to reach Java and join the Army of Independence. He looked at Don, Skinny and Roy.

"Are they Eurasians too?"

I nodded.

"Come with me."

We followed him into a strong, well-made hut, standing apart from the others, and he invited us to sit down on the rush mats that covered the earthen floor. He sat cross-legged opposite us, his hands on his knees.

"Are you the leader of the party?" He looked at me.

"Yes."

"From where you come?"

"From Medan."

"How come you so far south?"

I told him of our journey through Sumatra, of our privations and sickness, and of the help we had received at the various kampongs. Then I pointed to Roy.

"My friend is sick," I said. "Can you help him?"

"He is indeed very sick," he said. "He will die."

As he was speaking three natives entered the hut carrying four Indian-style rope-and-web beds which they rigged up across the corners. The headman saw me looking at them.

"It is best. Doubtless you wish to stay here for a while."

The natives padded out, and a few minutes later returned with food. It was a mixed curry of fish, yams and chicken, and after weeks of semi-starvation tasted almost too good to be true. But Roy ate nothing; he lay back, his eyes closed, breathing quickly. When we had finished the old man handed round cigarettes made from a bitter aromatic leaf. He seemed disposed to talk, and after I had asked the usual questions about the whereabouts of the nearest Japanese, I mentioned the soft green fruit we had eaten with such peculiar effects.

He smiled. "Ah, Obat Guna, the charm tree." And that was all he would tell us.

Before we settled down for the night I went to the door of the hut and asked a passing native for a bucket of water so that we could bathe Roy.

There is no feeling quite so terrible as looking at a dying man and knowing you cannot help him—especially if you've gone together through all the things we had. He was in a coma now, his eyelids half-closed, with the yellow that once was white filming over his shrunken pupils. We washed him carefully, then, leaving Skinny to watch him, Don and I turned in. At about midnight Skinny woke me, saying that Roy's breathing seemed to be normal and that he was in a deep sleep. I covered him with some extra clothing, then, while Skinny slept, watched and waited through the small hours of the night.

In the darkness of the atap hut I thought of the cost of our escape. Seventeen men had broken out; four were left, and one of them was dying. Absentmindedly I felt in the pocket of my shorts for the scrap of paper on which I had written down the members of our escape party. I had scrawled their names in pencil, but from heat and immersion in water they had almost all become obliterated. Obliterated like their owners I thought, all but four—or perhaps even now it was all but three. My thoughts turned to Pat's smiling face as she disappeared aboard the *Wakefield*. The last, I thought, I should ever see of her. And what of our child that never was? Oh, the cruelty and the tragedy of war.

We awoke next morning to the early bustle of natives moving about the kampong. After we had breakfasted the old man came in; he glanced at Roy, then rather sheepishly at me.

"You must move on," he said.

"But what of my friend? He can hardly walk."

"Your friend looks better. You must go."

I looked at him keenly, wondering what had brought about such a change of attitude.

"Can you tell us which way we should go?"

"If you wish to reach Java, you must go first to Oasthaven."

"But what of the Japanese?"

He shrugged his shoulders.

"Better not argue with him," muttered Don. "We don't want him to turn nasty."

So I thanked the old man as politely as I could for his hospitality and a little before noon we again set our on our interminable trek. For the first few miles we followed a faint pathway that ran eastward, parallel to the coast. There was a cool breeze from off the sea, freshening us and giving us new energy; energy we needed, for we had to take turns, two at a time, to carry Roy. Stumbling along, with long and frequent pauses, we made slow progress. That afternoon it rained steadily, and after one of the most miserable days I have ever endured, we found a sheltered spot underneath a cairn of rocks and camped down for the night. Roy was conscious, but only just. I knew that he was dying.

"Don," I whispered, "we can't go on like this. If we give ourselves up, at least Roy will get medical care; and perhaps the three of us can try later for another breakaway."

But Roy had heard me.

"What medical care would those yellow bastards give me?" he muttered weakly. "A bayonet in the guts, I'd rather take my chance with you."

And so we left it. He was a brave man.

That night his fever again flared up. There was nothing we could do, except take turns at staying at his side, watching as he struggled desperately for breath, sweating and shivering. His skin was hot to the touch.

At dawn he was still alive and I stayed with him while Don and Skinny went foraging for food. Looking from our hideout towards the misty sea, there was no sail, no living creature to be seen. Presently Don returned with some fruit and a handful of roots which we cleaned in sea water. Then we heard a shout, and coming along the shore was Skinny, grinning sheepishly; by his side was a native girl—a dark, sultry and attractive Chinese-Javanese of about eighteen. She was wearing what looked like black silk trousers and a lace baju.

"Trust the silly fool to find a skirt," whispered Don.

"Look what I've found," smirked Skinny.

"How the hell can you eat that?" grunted Don.

"Her name's Li-Tong." Skinny was quite unabashed. "I found her down by the shore."

I turned to the girl. "Where are you from?"

She pointed vaguely down the coast, then stood smiling at Skinny, who looked for all the world like an adolescent teenager introducing his first girlfriend to the family. I went up to the girl and pointed at

Roy.

"This man is ill. Can we get medicine at your kampong?"

She shrugged her shoulders.

"Maybe."

"Shall I go with her and find out?" Skinny offered, with alacrity.

"No, you damned well stay here," snapped Don.

"Let's take a chance," I said. "We'll all go."

Between us we picked up Roy and followed Li-Tong along the shore. After a couple of miles we came to a typical native fishing village, the huts erected on long bamboo poles below the high-water line and the nets placed underneath to trap the tidal catch of fish. This time our reception was not too friendly. The natives clustered together casting suspicious glances at us as we followed the girl towards the centre of the kampong. There we sat Roy down and stood around him. Li-Tong disappeared into one of the larger huts.

"Better not take any chances," I muttered to Don. "We'll stay here; the next move is theirs."

After a few minutes six men dressed in loincloths approached us. They were led by an elderly native, beside whom walked Li-Tong. I bowed and greeted him in the usual manner.

"Greetings, tuan."

"Where are you from?"

"From Medan."

"Why are you so far south?"

"We are trying to reach Java."

"Why do you come here? In the larger ports are many ships."

"And also many Japanese, tuan."

"Are you English?"

Remembering that his daughter Li-Tong was of mixed parentage, I decided on a little finesse.

"My friends are English. I am Eurasian."

"Why do you wish to go to Java?"

"My people are there."

"Why do you not travel alone, then? Your friends will only hinder you."

"Tuan," I said, "these friends are my true friends. They would die for me as other of my friends have died." I remembered the Koran. "Did not the Prophet say that good friends are as precious as all the wealth of the world?"

He looked at me closely.

"That was well spoken. Stay here if you wish, but I warn you we get many visits from the Jippon soldiers. All our men who do not fish have to work for the Japanese."

"Are they paid for their work?"

"Yes."

"Then I too will work for them. I can then pay for my friends."

"Are you not afraid?"

"Why should I be? The Japanese do not kill Eurasians."

"Welcome then to my home."

He turned, beckoning us to follow. He led the way into a dilapidated bamboo hut, while two natives carried Roy to another hut. I asked the old man if Roy would be looked after.

"We will treat him as best we can," he said. "But since the Jippon devils came our doctor tuan visits us no more."

Before settling down for the night, Don and I went over to Roy's hut, where we found two native women feeding him with a thick liquid, like brown vegetable. He took two wooden spoonfuls, then vomited it up. I crossed over to him, knelt by his side and asked how he felt. His forehead was moist with sweat and his eyes had that heavy-lidded stare that we had come to dread. He swallowed feebly, and whispered in a thin, remote voice that he was "OK."

Next morning he was hardly conscious and was muttering in delirium.

But I had other things to think of, for a little after daybreak I joined a party of fifteen kampong labourers bound for the Japanese working party. We were, it seemed, to be employed in building a coastal road. In charge of the sixteen of us was a foolish-looking Japanese sergeant.

We walked for some two miles before coming to an open space where a crowd of about a hundred men were already at work, digging a broad, shallow trench and lugging away the earth in bamboo baskets. Sitting in the shade of a dilapidated hut was the Japanese in charge. I stared at him. "This is it," I thought.

But it seemed that first I had to register for work with the foreman, a tall, likeable Sundanese. He looked at me, looked away and then looked back again. I told him my name was Oehlus and that I had been employed as an overseer at the estate of Tapakkanda (the district north of Medan). I thought that given reasonable luck this was a story I could get away with.

The foreman, who was dubbed "Biji" by the others, took me over to the Japanese. "Be careful, tuan," he muttered as we neared the atap hut. My nerves tingled.

The Japanese was true to type, arrogant and uncouth, with the air of lassitude brought about by having little work. He was thick and short, his eyes heavy-lidded. He spoke in a mixture of broken Malay-cum-Javanese.

"Where are you from?" The eternal question.

"Tuan," I said—it was a good opening gambit—"I have been employed as an overseer on a rubber estate called Tapakkanda near Medan."

"Why you leave?"

"My boss was Dutch. He evacuated and tried to make me go with him, but I slipped away."

"Why?"

"I wish to reach my family in Bandung."

"Why you stop here?"

"Tuan, I have no money."

"Why you not go with your Dutch boss?"

"Tuan, the great imperial army of Nippon promised on their wireless that Eastern peoples will soon be free. For many years I have wanted to be free from my Dutch boss." I spat on the ground.

He looked at me straight in the eyes.

My eyes are blue.

"Oehlus."

"Yes, tuan."

"You are not English?"

"No, tuan. Not English." Again I spat. "My father was German; my mother a Malay Eurasian." This was a story I had long prepared, but as I used it for the first time I had a sudden panic-stricken thought that the Jap might speak to me in German. But he only nodded.

"It is a good mixture." With that he entered my name on a sheaf of papers which he pushed into his tunic pocket and turned away.

That day I forgot I was a European. I acted like a Eurasian and spoke, when I had to speak, in Malay; and all the time I kept my eyes and ears open for signs of other Japanese who might be quicker on the uptake than the foolish sergeant in charge of our party. The work itself was hard and exhausting, especially to one in my physical condition. We dug the earth and gravel with spades, broke up docks with heavy hammers, and lugged the debris in heavy buckets of wood and bamboo to a mounting pile, well away from the ribbon of road that was beginning to take shape. At four o'clock we were told to stop, and rest was never more welcome. Covered with mud, I felt I looked as much a native as the others.

Late in the evening we were marched back to the kampong, where I found Don lolling miserably about.

"Have you eaten?" I asked him.

"Yes."

"OK. You and Skinny stick here; I'd better eat with the boys."

"Listen, Mac," he grunted. "Skinny's been out all day. I didn't see a sign of him till five minutes ago."

"Out all day? Where's he been?"

"Who knows?"

We stared at each other.

"How's Roy?"

"Slipping fast. I doubt if he'll last the night."

"Oh, God! And after all he's gone through ..."

At that moment Skinny came ambling through the doorway. I grabbed him by the shoulder.

"Look here, you stupid cuss, when I'm away, you stay here in the hut and don't damned well move."

"Take it easy, Mac. We're OK here."

"Two miles away," I told him, "I'm working for the Japs, trying to earn money to pay for our keep. One breath of suspicion, somebody'll talk and it's curtains for the lot of us. I'll not have you wandering about."

"OK, Mac, OK. But I can't stay indoor all day, can I? I gotta get some air." He grinned.

"Where've you been?"

"With Li-Tong and her pa."

"I thought so! Well, watch your step. We got out of Singapore and we've got his far. I'm not having you mucking things up at this stage. Understand?"

He understood.

Silently, without fuss, in the small hours of the tropical night, Roy died. It was a happy release. The words fall glibly perhaps, but that is exactly what it was—a happy release. For months he had been racked by pain, and sheer guts had pulled him through—nothing else. He had the heart and will of a lion.

We carried his thin, light body to a clearing outside the village, dug a grave for him, covered his body with ferns and buried him. We said the few prayers we knew; probably they were the wrong ones, but I do not think that mattered. We marked the spot with a rough bamboo cross, and there we left him.

We had known so little about Roy. Where did he come from? Was he married? Had he any children? About himself he had told us nothing. As we came away from the grave I felt the tears pricking against my eyes. I heard a voice I hardly recognized as my own muttering half-forgotten lines:

> "... There shall be
> In that rich earth a richer dust concealed
> A dust whom England bore, shaped, made aware
> Gave, once, her flowers to love, her ways to roam."

"Rupert Brooke," said Don.

"You know him?" I was astonished.

"Too true, cobber. Too true."

Chapter Eight

After we buried him we did not speak of Roy again. Death had been close to him so long that we had come to accept its shadow as our fifth companion, marching unseen beside us. The end had been inevitable; the instinct of self-preservation had forced a tough hide over our emotions; there was nothing we could do about it.

Later that morning the father of Li-Tong came to our hut and offered his condolences.

"We will look after your friend's grave," he said.

"Thank you." I could say no more.

"You will be leaving soon, tuan?"

I looked at him curiously, wondering what prompted the anxiety in his voice.

"Soon," I said. "I will work for the Japanese a little longer, then I can pay you for our stay here."

"That is what I wish to discuss, tuan. Tomorrow the Japanese sergeant will pay you for your work. Then you must go."

"But the Japanese will wonder where I've gone."

He shrugged his shoulders.

I tried another tack.

"Can you help us to cross the sea? Over the Sunda Strait to Java?"

"That would not be easy." The carefully expressionless face indicated that we could not expect much help.

"Listen," I said. "You cannot wish us to stay here. If the Japanese catch us, they would surely make us tell where we've been staying."

The implication went home. For a moment he sat quite still, then he rose, giving me a quick, hard look.

"Perhaps something can be arranged," he said, and walked thoughtfully towards his hut.

That day I again toiled through the enervating heat with the listless working party, and in the cool of the evening the Japanese sergeant handed me four and a half occupation guilders. These, on my return to the kampong, I handed over to the headman. He thanked me. Later he came across to our atap hut.

"Tuan, one of my friends is going fishing tonight; he will take you and the other tuan across the water to a small island."

I looked at him keenly.

"But we wish to reach Java. To be taken to an island would not help us much."

"My friend will take you to the island, tuan. His brother will then take you on to Java."

"Why can't he take us to Java himself?" I turned to Don. "No good getting stranded halfway," I muttered.

The old man looked at me with some annoyance. "Tuan," he sighed, "I will see what can be done." He went out. Then the significance of what he had said suddenly hit me.

"What's he talking about?" I muttered to Don. "He said his

friend would take me 'and the other tuan'. But there are three of us. Three tuans: you, Skinny and me."

"Guess you heard wrong, Mac."

We waited anxiously for nearly an hour, then back came the headman with his friend, a powerful, thickset fisherman.

"Tuan, this is the man who will take you and your friend to the island. His brother has a pukpuk boat which will pick you up from there and carry you to Java; it is too far for him to go himself."

There was no alternative but to accept his offer. At least we should be a step further on our journey, a step, albeit a small one, closer to Australia. Even if the worst happened and we were left stranded on the island, we could probably think up some way of getting ourselves off it. We had, after all, escaped from far worse situations.

"Thank you," I said to the headman. "We will go with your friend; but I have no more money to reward you with; I can only give you a letter, which you must hide until the Japanese are driven out; then you must show it to an English tuan who will give you money."

I turned to Don.

"Got anything I can write on?"

"Only a scrap of chocolate carton." Out of the tattered pocket of his shirt he produced a yellow, sweat-stained piece of cardboard and a stub of blue pencil.

On the back of the cardboard I wrote:

This village has today (I don't know the date) helped R. G. Donaldson (Australia), C. E. McCormac (Great Britain) and Chris Skinner (Great Britain) to leave Sumatra and further their escape from the Japanese. Please pay them a reward.

Don and I signed it, but Skinny held back.

"I don't think I ought to," he said.

"Why on earth not?"

He muttered something unintelligible and turned restlessly away.

"Come on, man. What's the matter with you?"

"Well, it's like this chaps. Reckon I'll stay behind."

"I knew it!" Don smacked a fist into his palm. "You poor, silly fool."

Skinny looked uncomfortable and shifted from one foot to the other.

"Well, this is how it is," he mumbled. "See, I've been doing a sort of line with Li-Tong and I reckoned I'd ask her to marry me."

"Well, for God's sake!" shouted Don. "You must be mad."

"Well, what's wrong with that?" Skinny muttered defiantly. "She's pretty and she's nice. You two can get along without me."

"But think of it, man," I pleaded. "You've always been grousing about living in the jungle; do you want to spend the rest of your life squatting under a lot of palm trees!"

Skinny began to look sulky.

"Well, I've made up my mind, and that's that."

"What about your folks?"

"That's my affair."

"Suppose the Japs catch you?"

"Don't worry. They won't."

It was fantastic. Far into the night we argued and argued, until at last the old man and the fisherman returned. They said they were ready.

Don and I each stuck a parang into our rough rope belts and

followed them out of the hut and down to the water's edge. It was raining steadily, with pale moonlight filtering through a layer of thin, diaphanous cloud. Drawn up on to the shelving beach was a sturdy ten-foot launch, with mast, sail and a small diesel engine. Skinny, with Li-Tong clutching nervously at his arm, followed us down to the water's edge. No one spoke, but as Don and I climbed over the gunwale, Skinny seemed suddenly to change his mind.

"Hold it! Hold it!" he shouted. "I'm coming too."

He started gesticulating to Li-Tong, lisping at her incoherently in broken Malay. She cottoned on pretty quickly, and at once started up a high-pitched wailing, clinging to his waist like a limpet. For several minutes there was pandemonium, with Li-Tong working up to a fine soprano shriek and Skinny jabbering away in a combination of broken Malay and choicest Anglo-Saxon. It was the old man who finally settled the argument. In one of the rare seconds of silence his thin voice quavered along the shore.

"If the Skinner tuan does not stay, the fisherman will not take the other tuans across the water."

Hurriedly I pushed off. "Looks like you've had it," I said.

I thought he would start another tirade, but Li-Tong nestled up to him and he seemed to recognize the inevitable. "OK then, reckon I'll have to stay."

"Suppose we get through," I asked him. "Whom shall I notify?"

"No one."

"What regiment were you in?"

He smiled artfully, "Signals."

The engine fired; in a gentle arc the launch drew away from Sumatra; the three of us waved until the coastline faded and the last we saw of Skinny was a tiny, rain-blurred figure, arms outstretched, stumbling into the little waves that lapped with heartless regularity onto the palm-fringed shore. Never have I been quite certain that our escape was not bought at the price of his captivity. What, I have often wondered, were his thoughts as the launch's outline faded into nothingness and he was left alone?"

But though of course we never saw Skinner again we did hear of him, and his story has a heartening postscript.

Towards the end of the Far Eastern war I found myself serving with SEAC Intelligence. Part of my duties was to interrogate personnel who had escaped through Japanese-occupied territory, and one day six Fleet Air Arm officers were brought to me for routine questioning. Theirs was a strange story. They had, it seemed, been taking part in a carrier-borne shipping strike against Jap merchantmen off Telok Betong. Opposition had been unexpectedly fierce and four Fireflies, badly damaged, had crash-landed in the jungle. One was never found, but the other three had managed to touch down in clearings and their crews had escaped serious injury. In each case the pilot and observer had hidden in the jungle for only a short time before they were contacted by natives, who had led them to a bearded white man. This white man, the officers said, was living like a king in a little fishing village on the south-east Sumatran coast. He had cared for them, entertaining them, and finally arranged for their safe transportation, via the "underground", back to Australia. Each of them could describe the white man and his wife in some detail. Obviously it was Skinny and Li-Tong. They were, I gathered, idyllically happy, with two children, an imposing bamboo atap hut and a small fishing vessel. The man had scorned the idea of returning to civilization, he was far too happy, he had said, where he was. So perhaps my qualms about our having left "the Skinner tuan" are without foundation.

We headed out to sea, and in soft, persistent rain the launch chugged southward into a dying ground-swell. Gradually the huddled figures on the Sumatran shore lost definition and merged into the darkness. Don and I sheltered from the rain under a layer of ragged coconut matting.

"Seventeen little nigger boys," I said. "Then there were two."

"There'd still be three," grunted Don, "if Skinny had a grain of sense."

We lay in the bottom of the boat listening to the slap of waves and the steady patter of rain. After about an hour the dark mass of an island took shape on our starboard bow; then dead ahead I made out the outline of another smaller island and soon our keel grated harshly onto a gravel beach.

"Where's this?" I asked the fisherman.

He only grunted and waved his hand towards the sombre rocky beach. "Wait here," he said.

"For how long?"

"Tonight."

We clambered out, our clothes sticking damply to our bodies, and as we made our way across the mud and stones of the beach to a protecting outcrop of rock, the taciturn native pushed off and, without another word, set course for Sumatra. We spent the night dozing fitfully in the shelter of the rocks, which offered some degree of protection against the driving rain. When we woke there was no sun and the sky was pewter-coloured and overcast. It was unpleasantly sticky and hot.

"We'd better not move," I said. "Cheerful Charlie's brother will expect us up here."

"If he ever comes," grunted Don.

We stayed by the beach for several hours but finally decided to explore the island, keeping the beach in sight. Climbing some twenty or thirty feet up the boulders, we looked down through a thin veil of mist on to a volcanic island two or three miles long. Over the water to the southward we were just able to discover the hazy outlines of another stretch of land.

On the eastern shore of our island were several fishing huts raised on stilts at the water's edge, but there was no sign of human life, which was hardly surprising as the vegetation was restricted to a handful of stunted shrubs which struggled with difficulty out of the barren rock. We search for food, but after an hour or so our sum total was only twelve berries, which tasted bitter and were therefore suspect, and a handful of anemic-looking roots. But in a natural hollow between the rocks we found a pool of water which did not taste over-salty.

About noon the mist cleared rapidly and we saw in the brilliant sunlight, only about a mile offshore, seven or eight Japanese flying boats, which seemed to be practising takeoffs and landings. Early in the afternoon a small naval vessel steamed past two or three hundred yards offshore and we could see the Japanese flag fluttering in the slow topic wind. Hour followed hour. At first I thought we might have been marooned but Don argued that with signs of Jap activity only a few hundred yards offshore our friends would not risk picking us up by day, but would wait for the coming of darkness.

He was right. About two hours after sunset, we heard the chug-

chug of an approaching launch; a few minutes later the boat nosed ashore, and we recognized our fisherman, and with him a younger man whom we took to be his brother. We waded out and climbed aboard.

"Boy, are we glad to see you!" grinned Don.

The younger native gave a non-committal grunt and started tinkering with the engine. After a few moments it speeded up and we again headed out to sea. After a long silence I tried to open the conversation.

"How do you manage to own a motorboat?"

"It belongs to the Japanese."

"How come you have it then?"

"I work for them. I look after the flying boat anchors." Obviously he meant buoys. I had a sudden idea.

"Are there many flying boats?"

Twelve or fifteen, perhaps."

"Are you taking us near them?"

Don realized what I had in mind. "Now don't start getting any damn silly ideas," he grunted.

"OK, cobber. But just think of the fun we'd have pulling the stoppers out of their hulls."

The elder fisherman motioned us to be silent. He leant over the port gunwale, listening. The distant purr of a motor-launch came whispering over the water. We were pushed into the bottom of the boat, covered with matting and told to keep silent—not that we needed any telling. After a few minutes the launch slowed down almost to a stop. We heard the muttering of voices, perhaps from a waterborne patrol; then we were again under way. Neither of the fishermen would tell us exactly what had happened, but we assumed we had met a Japanese patrol and the brothers had somehow convinced them of the harmless nature of our voyage. Shortly afterwards the engine was throttled back once more and in the gloom we could pick out the soft, waving branches of trees and palms. The launch nosed gently onto the sand.

"Java," said Cheerful Charlie.

He whispered a few words to his brother. "Wait," he said, and they vanished into the darkness.

"Not exactly a talkative couple, are they?" Don grunted as together we squatted on the shingle, some fifty yards from the launch.

"Why should they be? It's usually the people who've talked the least who've helped us the most. Except," I added, "for Nang Sen."

"I can't make out why they help us at all," muttered Don. "Much easier for 'em to stick a knife in our backs and claim the Jap reward."

"I know they're scared of the Japs; but maybe they're more scared of something else?"

"Such as?"

"This Army of Independence, perhaps."

After about an hour our two fishermen returned; with them was a Javanese, a surly, taciturn man. He seemed annoyed—not unreasonably I thought—at being dragged out of his bed.

"He will look after you now," said the elder brother. "We must go."

We shook hands with the fishermen, who were obviously anxious to be on their way, and watched their launch disappear into the darkness of Sunda Strait. Then we followed the Javanese. He led us through a tangled mass of mangroves into a belt of thick undergrowth which in turn gave way to an endless, swampy scrub. How he knew where he was going we were quite unable to fathom, for there seemed to be no defined track or path. On and on we went, until at last dawn broke in a flood of pale golden sunlight which shimmered in the countless pools and sparkled brightly on the dew-wet foliage. In the daylight we increased our pace through thickening vegetation. Our guide began to show signs of nervousness. We made good time for about three miles through scrubby secondary jungle; then quite suddenly came to a belt of dark, primeval forest. For about three hundred yards we followed a well-defined track. Then the Javanese stopped.

"Friends here," he said.

I looked around at the dank, impenetrable jungle.

"Where?"

He shrugged his shoulders and pointed down the track.

"What's the name of this place?"

"Merak."

He was a man of few words. He again pointed down the dark, hemmed-in trail. "Friends there. You walk." And he turned on his heel and strode rapidly away. Don and I looked at each other. Then we burst out laughing. Obviously we had no alternative but to follow his advice. We walked for about another mile, then found some fruit and, tired out, lay down to rest.

But we were stupid. We stretched out only a few yards from a gradual curve in the trail. We could not have chosen a less suitable spot. After our long run of luck we had perhaps become careless and less cautious. We had a good rest and were on the point of moving off again, when less than thirty yards away a man swung into view, walking rapidly towards us. Idiots that we were, we had loitered on a blind corner; he was almost bound to see us, and he carried a revolver.

Don dived into the undergrowth on the opposite side of the track. I froze motionless on the spot where we had been lying.

The man stopped; he took a few paces towards Don; I saw his finger curled over the trigger. He was a youngish man, black-haired and barefooted. His skin was burned brown from the sun, but it was not the brown of an Indonesian. He wore grey slacks and a whitish shirt. Obviously, I thought, a European. I watched uncertainly from my inadequate hideout.

"What are you two fairies doing here?" The voice had a rich, Australian twang. Its owner was entirely self-possessed. He waved his gun towards me.

"Out you come."

And out I came.

"You next" The gun circled round to Donaldson who scrambled ignominiously from underneath a thorn bush.

"Who the hell are you?" he muttered sheepishly.

"Who the hell are you?" The stranger had an air of definite authority. "If you want any help, maybe I can do something for you. I heard you were around. Where are you from?"

"Singapore," I said.

"I heard there was a big break there. Were you in it?"

"Yes," said Don. "Unless there was another."

"No, there was only one."

"You seem to know a lot." Don eyed him speculatively. But the stranger let the remark pass.

"Where are the rest of you?" he asked curtly.

"Dead," answered Don. "All except one, and his fate was worse than death."

"Torture?"

"No. He got married."

The stranger grinned. "Jesus," he drawled. "This is a terrible war."

"How did you know we were here?" I asked.

"We don't answer questions around here," he said. "We only ask them." He led us down the track. "Come on, we can talk while we're walking. I'm taking you to a chap who runs a guerrilla band."

We tried to find out who the stranger was and what exactly he was doing. But, once again, we met a curtain of silence and evasion. He spoke English like an Australian, and Javanese like an Indonesian. He talked laconically and with a dry wit, treating us to quaint and ribald remarks which he claimed were from Sheridan. But of himself, of his mission and of his guerrilla leader he told us precisely nothing.

For about three miles we followed him down the track. On either side the jungle became darker and more primeval; great trees, their trunks swathed with lichen moss, crowded closely together, the foliage far above us forming a canopy through which the sunlight filtered in pale green eddies. Quite suddenly we came to a clearing. Some twenty bivouac tents, their canvas camouflaged in a mosaic of green and brown, were grouped around the perimeter in the centre of the clearing; beneath the shadow of a giant palm, a handful of Indonesians were cleaning rifles. They watched with impassive detachment as we walked past them towards the largest of the tents.

Even that first morning I noticed about the guerrilla camp an air of watchfulness and mystery.

Chapter Nine

Our guide stopped outside the tent and shouted something in Dutch. The flap was at once pulled back and a tall, fair-haired man came out. He was dressed in the dark green uniform of a Dutch officer; a revolver strapped to his waist, and down the left side of his face an ugly scar jagged red from eye to lip. He spoke fluently in Dutch to our guide, who replied with equal rapidity in the same language, then turned to us, shook us warmly by the hand and without another word walked back along the track.

The scarred man eyed us coldly. He drew aside the flap of his tent, but the gesture was not one of hospitality. He spoke curtly.

"I'll take you first," he nodded at Don. "You," he stared at me, "can wait outside."

Don and I were interrogated, one after the other; and obviously our host was checking that our stories coincided. To me he said his name was Mansfeldt. He added that we could remain with his contingent for a while provided we behaved ourselves. He promised to hide us from the Japanese and, when the opportunity arose, to help us contact our own people; we in return had to agree to obey his orders implicitly.

Politically, he had very definite views. According to his line of reasoning, the British had been responsible for the fall of Java because, with Singapore represented as impregnable, the Dutch had not bothered to prepare the defences of Batavia or Surabaya. Politics weren't my concern, I told him; I was an airman; my job was simply to fight.

"So is mine," he said. "You'll see plenty of fighting if you stay with us. If you are wounded I'll do my best for you; but I'll not endanger the lives of my own men. Do you understand?"

"Fair enough," I said.

"You will have much work to do, but to start with I shall not allow you to operate with us in any of our skirmishes."

"How do you mean—operate?" I asked.

"Our task is to kill."

"Sounds the right idea to me. The only good Jap is a dead one."

He eyed me carefully. "That is true; and not only of the Japanese."

I made no comment and he rose and led the way outside, to where we found Donaldson whittling down a piece of wood with his parang.

"Nice friendly crowd you've got here," he said to Mansfeldt. "Not one of them has bothered even to say hello."

Mansfeldt only smiled.

"You'll be all right," he said. "Ask no questions, do as you're told, and …" his face twisted into the semblance of a smile, "… you may in time even come to like us!" And he led the way towards a group of the guerrillas. They were an odd-looking contingent, wearing shorts and either shirts or bajus. Some were barefooted, while others wore crudely made sandals—the only one with decent shoes was Mansfeldt, who sported pliable, well-cleaned calf-boots. As we approached, the guerrillas were busy cleaning and assembling a wide assortment of rifles, Tommy guns and revolvers, but one or two of them I noticed had parangs stuck in their belts. They were a mixed crowd of Dutch, Eurasians and Javanese, with a handful of Chinese and Mongolians, and we were introduced to them as Mister Donald and Mister Mac. When we got to know them properly what a grand bunch we found them to be! A collection of the most peculiar individualists, they were all working together for Mansfeldt under the strictest possible discipline; though exactly what they were working for was not at first apparent to us.

We stayed for several weeks with the guerrillas, content after the privation we had endured to relax in the company of an organized and purposeful band. Day after day we carried out the routine tasks assigned to us; weapon-cleaning, cooking, scouting and the like. Day after day we came into the closest physical contact with members of the guerrilla force; but of their personal hopes and fears, aspirations and desires we could discover nothing except that their first objective was to remain hidden from the Japanese. Several times we moved camp to avoid discovery, keeping to little-used pathways and moving always deeper into the vastness of the jungle.

Then early one morning Mansfeldt's scouts warned us, quite calmly, of an approaching Japanese patrol. We at once struck camp. There was no panic, though Don and I were secretly terrified. In next to no time, the tents were cleared away, packed together ready for instant transport and hidden in the undergrowth, while the forty-two of us melted in ones and twos into the jungle. Don and I were together, crouched behind a giant tree trunk, each of us clutching nervously at a well-sharpened parang. Very soon the first Jap came into sight—a squat, square-faced sergeant; he was followed by eighteen others in single file, carrying rifles with bayonets at the ready. They passed almost through the centre of the clearing, but so well had all traces of our camp been effaced that they noticed nothing, and padded away into the jungle with never a backward glance. After two or three minutes Mansfeldt's men began to emerge from their hideouts as unconcerned as if nothing had happened. The tents were re-erected and the routine of the camp quickly returned to normal. I asked one of the Eurasian guerrillas why Mansfeldt had taken no action, but he merely grinned and said that Mansfeldt knew what he was up to. To Don and me it was all completely mystifying.

During the days that followed, Don and I learned more about jungle fighting than we had ever thought possible. We learned to make our way through the thickest undergrowth without a sound; how to imitate the various bird calls that Mansfeldt's men used as signals; and a hundred and one other points about jungle survival which, had we known them before, would have saved us much hardship. The bird calls were in fact an elaborate code of signals, whereby a series of lookouts hidden in trees could pass back messages to the main body, all of whom by interpreting the calls would know exactly what was happening. As Don remarked late one evening, Tarzan had nothing on us.

"You know, Mac," he went on, "we were lucky in Sumatra."

"How come?"

"Well, just think of the noise we made—we must have sounded like a whole herd of elephants crashing through the jungle."

"We can do a bit better now," I agreed. "But I wish Mansfeldt would let us put our new technique to some use."

The next day, very early in the morning as layers of mist hung low over the sleeping jungle, we were told to assemble. We broke camp at once and this time Mansfeldt was in earnest. For five days we marched in a long straggling line weighted down with equipment. We travelled fast, sometimes by day, sometimes by night, heading eastward through a network of little-used jungle trails; often we covered thirty miles at a stretch. We followed Mansfeldt blindly, knowing nothing, asking no questions. On the afternoon of the fifth day we made a temporary camp, but erected no tents. A meal was prepared, then we slept. At last, as the sun was slipping low behind the tangled branches of the jungle, Mansfeldt left us, taking twenty-five of our number with him; the remainder, including Don and me, set out in a slightly different direction under Mansfeldt's second-in-command. At last, I thought, we were going into action. But the action when it came proved to be something of an anti-climax. Our party, it seemed, were to act as the decoy. We camped that night beside a small oval lake; for the first time in weeks we lit campfires, piling on dead branches and sun-dried grass until the flames danced brightly in reflection across the starlit waters; one of the Eurasians dropped a pile of enamel plates; there was much shouting and laughter.

Suddenly, from the opposite shore of the lake a crescendo of rifle-fire swept across a narrow jungle trail leading to our encampment. The Jap patrol which had been working expectantly towards us had themselves been ambushed; they were wiped out to a man. An hour later Mansfeldt returned, grimly satisfied. His only casualties were two wounded Javanese, one of whom was carried unconscious in a rough rope-spun hammock while the other with a bullet through his calf lurched after his comrades on a pair of primitive crutches.

Sentries were posted and in the light of our cooking-fires we settled down to a meal and to examining our spoils. There were a number of uniforms, a mass of rifles and a few automatic weapons. After a while Mansfeldt called Don and me over and gave us each a revolver, a box of ammunition, a pair of shorts and a roll of khaki-grey material which he suggested we wrapped like puttees round our legs. Don's revolver was of Dutch manufacture; mine was a Colt.

"Don't worry," said Mansfeldt, as we handled our weapons carefully and counted up the bullets, "I've got plenty more."

"But these are Dutch and American guns."

"That's right, we've just wiped out a Jap patrol and pinched their armour. That's the pièce de résistance over there." He pointed to a machine gun that a few yards away some of his men were already dismantling and cleaning.

"The Japs took them from our boys first. Now we've got 'em back again."

"And now you've given us guns I hope you'll give us the chance to use them?"

"Maybe."

A few days later my wish was granted, though once again we did not see a great deal of actual fighting—if fighting it could be called: it seemed to me more like indiscriminate slaughter. One evening in the short tropical twilight Don and I found ourselves lying on a well-wooded hill slope overlooking a small kampong which, according to Mansfeldt, was sheltering a Japanese patrol of twelve men. For a long while there was utter silence, then came a staccato hail of fire ripping from two directions into the flimsy atap huts. For about ten seconds there was a confused medley of screams and shouts, then all was quiet, deathly quiet. A few minutes later we heard a rustling through the undergrowth and Mansfeldt and his men came filtering back to the hilltop carrying several dozen boxes of ammunition in rope slings; with much satisfaction Mansfeldt told us that a Japanese patrol, billeted in the village, had been wiped out. Looking down on the silent kampong it was abundantly clear that every one of the inhabitants, both Japanese and Javanese, men, women, and children had, in the still tropical twilight, died in our murderous hail of cross fire.

"Serves the bastards right," Mansfeldt grunted. "They sheltered a Jap patrol. They refused us food. They were non-cooperative."

"Why should they want to help you?" I was angry and disillusioned. "They only wanted to be left in peace. It was plain murder."

"It was war."

"What did those children know of war?" Don broke in. "You killed them needlessly. In cold blood."

Mansfeldt sighed. "Do not meddle, Englishman, in things that don't concern you. There are in Java more wars than one."

Such incidents, I realize in retrospect, were the birth pangs of the movement for Indonesian Independence.

"You may in time almost come to like us," Mansfeldt had said, but the longer Don and I stayed with his guerrillas, the less we liked the way they operated. We began to look forward eagerly to the day when Mansfeldt would fulfil his promise and put us in touch with our own people; but as week followed week, with no mention being made of our moving on, we grew dispirited and apathetic. To start with, we several times discussed the idea of leaving the guerrillas and striking off by ourselves into the jungle; but for a variety of reasons we never took the final step. Eventually we came to drift along in a listless mental stupor, as though we no longer had a purpose in living, but were content merely to exist from day to day. Was it, I wonder, because we had developed into a pair of animals, happy so long as we could feed and sleep? Was it a sort of physical and mental anemia resulting from the weeks we had spent with no food other than berries and jungle fruit? Or was it because we had seen death so often and so close that this new life, with its utter dependence upon Mansfeldt, came now as a way of escape from the problems we had faced hitherto? A psycho-analyst could doubtless puzzle it out and pronounce some clever judgment as to what we should have done; but the fact remains that for several weeks we accepted our strange way of life with resignation.

Then at last the longed-for day arrived. About three weeks after the attack on the kampong, Mansfeldt called Don and me over to his tent. He was working on a small portable radio receiver and transmitter. As we entered he took off the headphones.

"You are leaving us at once," he said curtly.

"And about time too," grunted Don.

Mansfeldt looked at him as though he had crawled out of a very small hole, and Don, shifting uneasily, dropped his eyes.

"This man," Mansfeldt went on coldly, "will be your guide. You will do precisely as he tells you. If you disobey him you will die."

Somewhat apprehensively I weighed up our guide. He was a formidable-looking Indonesian, well over six feet tall, clearly not the sort of man to be trifled with.

"Where will he take us?" I asked.

"Englishman, you are slow to learn. You have a proverb, I believe: Ask no questions and be told no lies."

"Yes, and we have another. Only a fool jumps out of the frying pan into the fire. Perhaps we'd rather stay with you."

"Perhaps so; but nevertheless you will go. Hand me your guns."

There was nothing we could do. Reluctantly we handed over our revolvers and ammunition. We had a last hurried meal with the guerrillas, then early in the afternoon I returned by myself to Mansfeldt's tent. I thanked him for harbouring us safely during the preceding weeks. He thought I was going to ask again where our guide would lead us, but deliberately I refrained. He seemed embarrassed and ill at ease.

"Do not thank me," he said stiffly. "The Japanese are my enemy as much as yours. I have no wish for them to capture you."

We shook hands.

As I turned to leave the tent he spoke more gently than usual. "Follow my guide, Englishman. He will take you to your own people." He sighed deeply. "It is not right that a man be cut off for too long from his own."

When we left, in the full blaze of afternoon, the guerrillas were camped in just such a clearing as that in which we had first contacted them. Still the air of mystery and watchfulness hung over the encampment and over the tall, scar-faced man who stood silently watching, as behind our Indonesian guide Don and I headed southward down an indeterminate jungle trail.

As first we had the greatest difficulty in keeping pace with the tall, long-legged Indonesian. He seemed motivated by a single purpose—to put as great a distance between ourselves and Mansfeldt as he could. Certainly he knew where he was going; for even when, late in the evening, we came to a swamp or met what seemed to be an impenetrable wall of jungle, he was never in the slightest doubt as to which direction we should take. To begin with we could find no point of amicable contact with him. He was remote and surly by nature, and his insularity seemed to us aggravated by the fact that I could hardly understand a word he said. He spoke in a guttural jargon that contained only a faint smattering of Malay, and in the end we were forced to adopt a sign language which at least enabled us to understand each other better.

That first day we loped along behind him with hardly a word spoken. Not that we had much breath for conversation, since he set a killing pace, and every time I indicated that Don and I wished to rest or eat, he would start to jabber angrily and stride off, even more rapidly, down the trail. We had, he knew, to follow. Soon, in the moist, sticky heat, we were covered in sweat and surrounded by a loathsome plague of flies. Not until darkness had closed completely round us did we halt, only to fall almost instantly asleep at the base of a giant tree some thirty yards off the trail. Next morning our guide woke us an hour before sunrise. Our bodies were stiff and aching and we longed for a substantial meal; but not for us the leisurely breakfast and the pleasant postprandial stroll. With gestures of impatience and grunts of annoyance our guide hustled us onto the trail and our nightmare progress was renewed. That day we must have covered close on fifty miles, with our only rest a half-hour's break for a hurried meal of yams and durians.

Exhausted as we were, the beauty of the country through which we travelled made only a blurred impression. As we progressed southeastward—still at the same fantastic pace—the jungle gradually thinned, and on our left the foothills of a mountain chain swelled up in gentle undulations across the eastern horizon. A number of clear, fast-flowing streams cascaded down from the hills, fanning out as they crossed the trail, then contracting again into narrow ravines as they fell away into the jungle on our right. The country seemed almost uninhabited except for a small number of birds, a very occasional kampong, which we carefully avoided, and of course the inevitable and ubiquitous flies.

Lulled by our isolation, we gradually came to lose any feeling of time, or, for that matter, any feeling of fear. It was as though we were being whirled along in a world of unreality where the usual things of life concerned us no longer. Our only thought was to keep up with our silent guide; our only hope that the journey would soon end. We had given up, long ago, any hope of being told where we were going—though at first we had hoped, almost every hour, that we were about to be put in touch with some of our own guerrilla forces, or at least with someone who could help us on the last lap of our two-thousand-mile trek to Australia. But as day followed day without our coming into contact with any living creature, Don and I began to live for the moment only.

About the ninth day, we broke into open, completely flat country. In the distance was an aerodrome and we watched the Jap planes landing and taking off directly overhead. Much to our consternation our guide headed directly towards the landing field.

"This is no place for us," Don said.

"Suppose not. But I'd like to pay a nice social call ... with a hacksaw!"

Only a few hundred yards from the perimeter of the airfield, which seemed to be completely unguarded, our guide slowed down and began to tread warily. We noticed that tree branches had been broken off, and debris was scattered over the track. Suddenly I spotted an aircraft, tilted crazily on its side, one of its wing crumpled and splintered. It was a Zero. Carefully we skirted round it until I could see quite plainly the pilot still strapped into his cockpit. He was dead.

We hurried away and almost at once came to a railway line which seemed to emerge from out of the aerodrome. Our guide, whom we had christened Roger, shinned up one of the tallest trees whose foliage made a fifty-foot-high canopy over the tangled undergrowth around us; he waved from the top, indicating that the line seemed to run east and west.

"This is not much good," I muttered to Don. "Surely we ought to try and reach the south coast. If we hop on a train here we might land up in Batavia or God knows where."

Our guide slithered down the tree, his bare feet miraculously finding tiny protuberances on the bark; he pointed agitatedly down the track and hurriedly dived for cover. We followed him into the undergrowth just as a troop train, belching smoke, snorted round the bend; its trucks were crammed with Japanese in grey-green uniform, their caps pulled low over their eyes. Anxiously we watched from beneath the sheltering leaves and did not stir until the thunder of the train died away, and only the chorus of jungle birds broke the evening silence. Daylight by now had almost vanished and we decided to camp down for the night close to the track.

About two hours after dark, in the steamy heat that blanketed the jungle with a thin layer of mist, we heard the clang and rattle of another approaching train. Emboldened by the darkness, we left our hideout, and took up positions beside the track, staring at the trucks as they lumbered slowly by. They seemed to be empty. Our guide seemed to make up his mind on the spur of the moment and gesticulated at the train, waving us towards it. We broke into a jogging trot, keeping pace with the trucks. Then, as the last one came alongside, we jumped at it independently, gripped the top edge of its wooden side and clambered aboard. Inside were only a few planks of timber and a couple of packing crates. Throughout the short tropical night, one of us kept watch, while the others dozed off, every now and then jolted into sudden wakefulness as the train clattered over a bridge or lurched perilously round a sudden bend. A little before dawn Don wakened Roger and me as the train, approaching a built-up area, slowed down. We jumped off it hurriedly, rolling down a small embankment into the shelter of the undergrowth.

Beneath the level of the track, our guide told us to wait, while he disappeared into the secondary jungle. He returned almost at once and indicated the route we were to take. Clearly he wanted to skirt round the town we had been approaching.

We struck off westerly, through a jungle track that ran at the foot of a range of mountains. These we kept on our left for the rest of that day and throughout the next morning. Midday saw us still loping along, rarely speaking, behind the guide, while the sun patterned the undergrowth into a mosaic of brilliant colour and spattered shade. Suddenly, without warning, the guide dropped to his knees, Don and I almost piling up on top of him. He pointed through a belt of undergrowth. The track curved sharply to the left, then led straight into a clearing, at the far end of which was a familiar cordon of wire, surrounding a Jap concentration camp. Inside there were the usual wooden, straw-roofed huts, and sitting about here and there a number of Europeans, both men and women. Jap guards were positioned at intervals, lolling listlessly about, rifles between their knees.

"Lord," muttered Don. "We almost walked into that one."

"Look over there!" I pointed to a patch of open ground beside the guard hut where three or four European women in flowered, cotton dresses were strolling about outside the wire, apparently free to come and go as they pleased.

"Not much point keeping them inside the cage," said Don. "They couldn't get far in this jungle."

"Malingping," said our monosyllabic guide.

"Malingping!" I repeated. Then, to Don, "Malingping's pretty near the south coast!"

Anxious quickly to leave the danger behind us, we crawled away on our bellies to the left of the encampment until we were far enough away to chance walking again. Then on and on we went, with the mountains still on our left. We continued throughout the day and, with only short pauses for water when we came to a stream, throughout the night too. We camped down next morning and rested until noon, then on again until midnight, when we slept for four or five hours.

We had covered only a couple of miles the next day when, in the grey light of dawn, we saw the sea.

Gripping us now was a new excitement. Neither of us spoke of it, but we knew it was there, a deep underlying tightening of the nerves. For we realized that the end might not be far away. We were on the south coast of Java travelling east. Every mile we covered was a mile nearer freedom. Our nerves were taut, because we were in a Jap-infested country, because liberty was near and because, after months of living by our instincts, running like wild animals from every sign of civilization, we were scared that the net might yet close over us. We were impatient with one another. Conversation lapsed and, even when we camped down for sleep, we spoke hardly at all. The final escape was becoming an obsession. Once again we had become filthy and bearded, our hair straggling loosely round our ears, our skins burned a dirty brown from the sun. Into Donaldson's pale blue eyes there crept a fierce, hunted look. The same look must have been in my own eyes. Nothing must stop us now. Nothing. We became surly with each other and with the Javanese guide.

Perhaps he sensed our thoughts, for that day he did not stop at sunset but pushed on until we came to a fishing village. Strangely enough the Javanese showed little interest in us as behind our guide we strode purposefully through their kampong. We slept the night in the centre of the village in a hut whose disintegrating wooden walls were saturated with the stench of fish; and there was fish for breakfast the next morning. I tried to draw the headman into conversation, but he was almost unapproachable. All I could get out of him was a taciturn "You will be taken on from here." We did not have to wait long. Half an hour later he came over to us and indicated that we were to follow him. He took us quickly to the water's edge where we saw a fishing boat bobbing up and down in the light swell of the surf, with eight Javanese crewmen, dressed in loincloths, holding it steady in the water. It was about twenty-five feet long, built on the lines of a Chinese junk, with a single mast but with an outrigger for stability. Don and I waded out to it, jumped aboard and were followed by our guide. We were pushed off and almost at once the swell lifted us out into the open sea

"Where the devil are they taking us now," muttered Don querulously. "There's no friendly land for a thousand miles!"

I shrugged my shoulders, and approached Roger as tactfully as I could. He knew what was in my mind and pointed shorewards.

"Jipponese," he said.

That was enough.

The whole of that day we headed towards the east, maintaining a course parallel to the coast and about two miles out. At nightfall the boat nosed towards land and we ran into another fishing kampong, hemmed in by a thick wall of jungle. We again spent the night in a fishing hut, and were again accepted by the villagers without the slightest spark of interest, as though the arrival of dishevelled Europeans was part of their daily routine. Staring out from the entrance to our hut, Don and I were uneasy.

"These blighters are an odd lot," I whispered. "What do you make of them?"

"They seem to be under orders," grunted Don. "As though they've been told about us and know exactly what to do."

"Do you think we can trust 'em?"

"We've got no alternative."

"They might be part of Mansfeldt's setup."

"Could be. But if so why don't they open up a bit?"

"Ease up, Don. You're getting edgy." But it was a case of the pot and the kettle.

We were just settling down for the night when a young Javanese, dressed in singlet and loincloth, came into the hut. He was carrying a small parcel.

"Hello there," he said, in a clipped Australian accent. "I speak English a little."

"Well, for crying out loud!" shouted Don. "Where on earth have you sprung from?"

He smiled inscrutably.

I introduced myself and Donaldson.

"Where are we?" I asked. "And where are we going to?"

"This village is called Bangsang," he replied. The second part of my question he pointedly ignored. I thanked him for his hospitality but told him that we couldn't understand why his people were helping us so much but would give no indication of they whys and wherefores. He smiled.

"The white tuan said you were to be taken care of. That is all you need to know."

"The white tuan?"

He pointed towards the east.

"You will meet him soon. He is a good man."

I looked at Don. "Feel better?" I asked. He grinned.

I asked the Javanese if there were many Japs along this southern coast.

"Yes, very many," he replied. "Most of them guard the white prisoners in camps."

"Where are the camps?"

"There are two less than thirty miles away."

"Are they camps for soldiers or civilians?"

"For soldiers and airmen—mostly airmen."

"English or Dutch?"

"English mostly, and ..." he spat on the floor, "a few Dutch, too."

I looked at him curiously. "You don't like the Dutch?"

"No."

A feeling of tension spread through the atap hut. To lessen it he began to unwrap the paper round the parcel he was holding. A small metal tin fell to the floor.

"Mac!" Donaldson's voice was almost reverent. "It's bully!"

"Bully?" I grabbed foolishly at the familiarly shaped tin. It was the usual service ration of corned beef. Don slapped the Javanese on the back, and began to open up the tin. Seeing our preoccupation the Javanese pulled out of his loincloth a slip of paper which he handed to me with a broad grin. Don peering at it over my shoulder, read out loud the pencilled words:

YOU WILL DO EXACTLY AS YOU ARE TOLD. BE SEEING YOU.

"Yours sincerely, Professor Moriarty!" said Don.

I turned to the Javanese. "Who gave you this?"

"The white tuan."

"Where is he?"

"You will see him soon. In a few days perhaps." He bade us good night and left us.

Opportunists as we had become, Don and I, without saying a word, disposed of the corned beef in less than five minutes, finally licking the remaining shreds of meat from off our parangs. The taste of it brought back nostalgic memories of civilization and mess-room meals. We lay on the floor of the hut, chatting animatedly, our spirits raised by this sudden change in our fortunes. But sober thoughts intruded, thoughts of some last-minute slip—a Jap raid on the kampong, perhaps, or an unexpected betrayal, or some chance encounter with a Jap patrol. We hardly slept at all, willing the night to end so that we could felt the nervy jab of frustration. Next morning we were again tired, irritable and keyed up. Dawn had hardly filtered away the last grey hour of night before Don was padding about the hut, nervously walking over to the doorway, then back again, scratching at his beard and muttering to himself like an old woman waiting for the longed-for postman.

"Take it easy, cobber," I said. "You won't get any forrader doing that."

"My God, Mac," he grunted. "Why don't they get a move on? I want to get cracking."

Back to the door he went, to and fro, back and forward, until I felt like screaming at him. For my feelings were the same as his.

We again breakfasted on fish, and at long last Roger came for us and led us down to the boat where the same crew were waiting. There was no sign of the Javanese who had spoken to us the night before. We pushed off, stood out to sea for a couple of miles, then hoisted sail and turned to port so that the boat again ran parallel to the shore, but well out to sea. At midday we fed off dried fish and rice, and drank tepid water from a small tank. The sun was hot throughout the long afternoon. Most of the others took cover under a straw canopy in the stern; but Don and I spent the whole time leaning on the gunwale, staring at the coastline, trying to spot signs of civilization against the deep purple of the jungle and the climbing blue of the mountains beyond. The Javanese watched us but said nothing.

About five in the evening, the helmsman altered course to port and we headed for another kampong whose huts, lifting out of the water on their stilts, took shape as we drew near. But this was a kampong we were never to set foot in. A few hundred yards offshore the crew started jabbering excitedly; there was a staccato exclamation from the helmsman and he pulled the tiller sharply across. We again headed straight out to sea, moving fast.

"What goes on?" I grunted.

Our Javanese guide jerked his thumb towards the shore. "Jipponese," he said.

I wondered how he knew, for staring back into the darkening line of shore, I could no sign of life. Perhaps that was how he knew that Japs were there—the villagers had vanished. I looked across at Don, who was leaning out low over the water from the gunwale opposite. The sweat on his forehead caught the last rays of the sun setting on our beams. He glanced over at me, with a nervous grin.

"Near thing, Mac," he said.

The man at the helm did not alter course until we were far out to sea. Then, at a safe distance, he again steered parallel to the coast. Some way ahead I could see the outline of what seemed to be a seaport and, anchored round it, a number of large ships. I asked Roger its name.

"Chilachap," he said.

Not far from the harbour entrance we drew in to a small island (I believe it was Kambangan) where the crew bought rice and fish from the villagers of a tiny kampong. We spent the night sleeping close to our boat, and left before dawn. As the sun came up, we were far out to sea and out of sight of land. That day was our last in the fishing boat.

Towards dusk the crew took us close inshore and, moving slowly eastwards, we sailed just outside the line of breaking surf while our crew stared hard at the coastline, looking for landmarks. Don and I stared with them but could see nothing but jungle and, beyond the jungle, the solid mass of the mountains. But finally the boat turned in straight, it seemed, for the exact spot the Javanese had been looking for. They seemed highly delighted with their navigation.

We spent the night ashore, not in a kampong, but under cover of the jungle, and early the next morning, while we were still asleep, the fishermen sailed away, leaving behind Don, Roger and myself.

The next three days were almost an anti-climax. We took to the jungle again, loping along much as we had done for so many months, keeping to the undergrowth, sleeping in the undergrowth, following an ill-defined track on the lower slopes of the mountains, with now and then a glimpse of the sea on our right. Continually in our ears was the background music of the jungle—a chant, in a thousand different voices, of a tune which once frightening, was now the overture to freedom, the tuning-up of the orchestra before it crashed into the majestic chords of a final crescendo. "God, and it please you God," I prayed, "don't let anything go wrong now."

On the afternoon of the third day we left the track and followed our guide to a point on the shore where, as if by a miracle, we found a small boat lying on its side secured to a bamboo stake driven deeply into the sand. It carried a short mast and a single lug-sail. We climbed in, pushed off and under a stiff wind sped fast across the water towards a pattern of islands. A little after moonrise we felt the grate of a gravel shore under the boat's keel. For a moment there was silence, then out of the darkness came a great voice, echoing around the sheltered cove.

"Come on you two! Over here."

Roger was already pushing off the boat.

"Aren't you coming too?" I asked him.

"There are things it is better not to see." He shook us by the hand. "You are safe now—the tuan will care for you."

Again the voice boomed out from the bottom of a low, precipitous cliff.

"Come on! Hurry!"

In the pale, shadow-casting light of the moon we stumbled over an outcrop of small, slippery rocks towards a cleft in the cliff. Between two enormous boulders was the entrance to a natural shelter. A hand grabbed us by the shoulder and guided us through the opening, a blanket was dropped behind us, an oil lamp was lit, and there in his Aladdin-like cave sat the tuan.

Chapter Ten

He was a short man; thickset, dark-haired and sun-burned. He was wearing a khaki-green shirt and shorts and a pair of rope-soled shoes. Behind him, in an alcove of the cave, stood a wireless receiver and transmitter, also a rack of rifles and Tommy guns.

"Hello there!" The accent was a deep Australian bass. "I was wondering when you two birds would turn up."

We stared at him, overcome with an inexplicable shyness. He was the first member of our Forces we had seen for five months. "Hi ya, cobber," muttered Don.

Emotion was welling up inside me. I could have grabbed him by the shoulders and cried and cried and cried; but all I did was to stare, and my mouth hanging foolishly open.

"Where have you come from?" His voice was deep, but kindly and reassuring.

"Singapore," I muttered.

"Do you, by God!"

Jerkily, I started to tell our story in a flood of incoherent words, but he held up his hand.

"OK, cobber, let it wait. There's plenty of time. You get some grub inside you first."

And we settled down to the most incredible of meals—tinned tongue and sausage, new potatoes and peas, followed by tinned pineapple and tinned cream.

Afterwards, relaxed and at east, I was all for continuing our story; but again the Australian stopped me.

"Look, chum, you two need sleep. So do I. I'll radio Darwin, then we can turn in."

"Darwin," Don muttered incoherently. "I reckon it's all a dream."

"Don't you believe it, chum. They're expecting you."

"Darwin," he muttered again. "Darwin! By God, Mac, we've really made it!"

"OK, chum. Take it easy." He pushed us gently into a narrow recess where he had hung for each of us a rope bunk slung from the natural ceiling. We lay far back, too excited to sleep, while he tuned up his transmitter; then after a few minutes we heard him tapping swiftly on a Morse key. Presently he looked in on us.

"You'll be OK. They're coming to pick you up."

We slept, deeply and serenely, for almost the first time in more than six months.

Next morning, we awoke refreshed, and full of questions for the Australian "tuan"—his name he refused to divulge.

"Just what are you doing here?" I asked him.

"Keeping an eye on our interests."

"What interests?"

He looked at me reproachfully. "All you need to know, chum, is that I'm here to help people like you."

I quickly changed the subject.

"When d'you reckon they'll come for us?"

"When they can. Maybe a couple of days. Maybe a couple of weeks. Now tell me about yourselves."

We told him, in as much detail as we could, and it took us most of the morning. He seemed particularly interested in our description of the Japanese flying boats at Oasthaven.

"H'm. We must try and clip their wings," he said.

I asked him if there were many Jap prison camps along the coast.

"Yes, quite a few. Most of the service types have been sent to Malaya and Borneo though; all that's left behind are women, children and a handful of men. Up north there are camps crowded out with RAF fellows, but we can't help 'em yet."

"Are there many Japs near here?" Don jerked in.

"Enough for you two wallahs to stay under cover all day."

Early that afternoon he left us and did not return until late at night. Don and I were left on our own with strict instructions to remain in hiding. It took all our patience to stay inside the hideout. Time passed slowly though we dozed off for about two hours in the steamy heat of the afternoon. From a couple of natives who came early that evening, we gathered that the Australian was not entirely on his own, but had a small band of Javanese working for him who busied themselves in the tiny camp hidden away in the rocks, or in the fishing kampong which we could see a few hundred yards away down on the water's edge. When our host returned from whatever mysterious errand he had been concerned with, I asked him point-blank who he was and who he was working for.

"Does it matter?" he answered.

"Perhaps not, but I'd like to know."

"You can call me what you like."

"Are you working on your own?"

"For a while, yes. But probably I'll be leaving soon. Things are getting a bit hot here. By the way," he added casually, "you two are being picked up tonight if the weather holds."

"Tonight!" It was almost too good to be true.

"That's the idea. In another five or six hours a seaplane is landing with supplies. They'll take you back to Darwin."

"Darwin," muttered Don. "By God, Mac, we really have made it!"

But fate had one last trick in store. That night, a few hours after dark, a violent tropical storm came sweeping out of the west; rain fell in torrents throughout the small hours of the morning, the thunder reverberating deep into the mountains behind us. Next morning it was hot and close and a thick mist blotted out the sea. At midday distant thunder again rolled among the hills, as the storm hovered between mountains and sea, circling around us throughout the whole day and the following night. Don and I became increasingly nervous. Sometimes thunderclaps cracked across the sky with so vicious an explosion that we expected the mountains to fall on top of us, burying us at the very last second of our bid for freedom. At other times, as for a few hours the storm eased off, we fidgeted about and plagued our host for news. We were getting worried now. Something was wrong. Fate had stepped in and was laughing at us, openly and derisively. Fools that we were to think we had escaped the net. We would never leave the shelter alive. Under cover of the storm the Japanese would come. So near and yet so far.

There was something almost supernatural about that storm. It hovered malignantly above us, increasing and decreasing in intensity, not for a single day and night, but for ninety-six hours.

Sometimes the Australian stayed with us and we yarned together in his Aladdin-like cave; at other times he disappeared on his own affairs, God alone knew where, and Don and I were left by ourselves, with our disturbing thoughts—terrified that even now our escape would be ended by a Japanese bayonet. Day after day the tension grew, as rain fell steadily from a leaden sky and thunder rolled among the coastal hills. The strain was beginning to tell on us. Thin of body, hardly speaking to one another, we could not sleep but lay awake tossing and turning on our improvised bunks.

But on the fifth night the weather suddenly cleared. There was no moon, but stars glittered brightly in the wide vault of sky. The Australian, who had been listening in to his radio for some hours, suddenly got to his feet.

"Get ready, chaps; this is it," he said.

He went outside, shouted orders to the Javanese over in the kampong, then came back and told us to follow him closely. He led us down to the water's edge, where the boat we had arrived in was riding quietly at its mooring. A Javanese crew of three fishermen came running from the kampong; they clambered in the boat and began to unfurl its single sail. We waded into the surf, jumped aboard and in a few seconds were standing out to sea. The Australian remained on shore.

"Do exactly as you're told," he shouted, as we waved goodbye.

Gradually the outline of his figure blurred into the darkness, but long after he was lost from sight his deep voice echoed out across the starlit water.

"Lucky bastards," were the last words we heard. "Crack a bottle for me when you get to Darwin."

The fishermen headed our boat straight out to sea. After about three hours they lowered sail, then threw over the anchor. Don was getting impatient.

"What the hell's happening now?" he growled.

Quietly a Javanese turned to me. "Wait, tuan," he said. "And be silent."

Very carefully and deliberately two of the Javanese threw a couple of long lines into the water and placidly began to fish.

Don's nerves were all on edge. He held his head in his cupped hands. "Fishing!" he muttered hysterically. "My God, Mac! Fishing! We've walked twelve hundred miles to join a bloody fishing trip."

"Quiet, tuan," whispered a Javanese.

Minute after minute, hour after hour the fishermen sat contentedly, watching their lines, occasionally drawing them in to unhook tiny silvery fish from off the pointed barbs. Don and sat there watching in frustrated exasperation. The Javanese took not the slightest notice of us. There was no sound but the slap, slap of water against the wooden hull. And on the bottom boards the pile of silver fish grew steadily in height. We could do nothing but sit and watch, forced into passive inertness when every nerve in our bodies was crying out for action.

One hour passed, then another. Don had slumped into semi-doze, his head in his hands, while I was leaning over the gunwale staring in deep water on the surface of which the stars were dancing in reflection.

Suddenly Don jerked his head up.

"What's that?" He was listening hard.

And then I heard it too—the distant drone of an aircraft. Becoming louder. Unhurriedly the fishermen pulled in their lines and sat quietly waiting. The engines roared nearer, but we could see nothing. The aircraft seemed to pass over us, then turn and again head out to sea. The deep hum faded. Behind me in the boat I heard a metallic click, and twisting round saw that one of the Javanese had produced a pocket torch which he was holding away from his body so that its spotlight was shielded from the shore. He waved the beam to and fro twice, then switched it off; after half a minute he repeated the signal. The engine-hum again increased in volume. Suddenly a fast-moving light flashed overhead and we could see, silhouetted against the starry sky, the vast, shadowy bulk of a flying boat. The engines were throttled back, and about half a mile away two powerful beams of light flicked low over the sea. Straining our ears and eyes, we heard the soft swish of rushing water as the aircraft ploughed towards our torchlight.

"Australia, here we come!" I muttered breathlessly to Don. My loincloth was sticking to me from the sweat running down my chest and my back. I was breathing quickly. My heart was pounding. My mouth was dry.

The two bright, staring eyes approached rapidly, then flicked off as the dark bulk of the Sunderland drew near us, the white curl of sea writhing away from its hull. Then it was alongside and our little boat bumped up against the metal hull.

"Mac, I'll love flying boats till I die," breathed Don.

There was the chink of metal from the side of the aircraft, a door opened and a man in khaki shorts leaned out, framed sharply against the light.

An Australian voice cut across the velvet water. "Unload these crates, you men, and make it snappy."

"Which crates?" I shouted back.

"Who's that?" There was a startled note in the voice.

"May we come in?" said Don.

"Hey skipper, what goes on?" The man turned away, glancing forrard. A second later another figure appeared by his side.

"Are you the two fellows we're taking back?" he asked.

"You bet we are."

"OK, hurry aboard."

Swinging one foot over the gunwale, Don pulled himself up by an iron rung. I scrambled after him into the vast riveted hull and together we crawled unsteadily towards a bunk. We sat on the grey woollen blankets, blinking in the strong light and staring back at the Australian faces that were gazing down at us. For several minutes two airmen stood by the door passing out parcels and crates to the natives, then the door was slammed and bolted. The throttle opened up, there was a quick rush of water, mounting in volume, followed by a gentle swaying, and then silence. The flying boat lifted into the tropical light. The vibration stopped and we smoothed ahead with only that empty-stomach feeling that comes from knowing there is nothing below you. I felt a little sick. A man whom the others called Tiny bent low and squirmed his way into the belly of the aircraft, returning with a bottle of brandy and a couple of glasses.

"Can you two jokers use some of this?"

"Too true," I said, and Don and I gulped the burning liquid down.

"Skipper says you've come a long way. Where are you from?"

"Singapore."

He looked at me with mingled curiosity and awe.

"What's the date?" I asked.

"The date? Why, Tuesday the sixteenth."

"Sixteenth of what?"

"September, of course. What d'you think it was?"

"We didn't know, cobber," said Don. "Papers weren't delivered in the jungle."

September. More than five months after the break-out from Pasir Panjang!

"We ought to parade you two scarecrows through Darwin," said Tiny thoughtfully.

Don and I filled our glasses again. We looked at one another. His eyes were wet, and I felt tears welling up into my own. Then I could control it no longer; the pent-up emotion overflowed, and I sat there my head between my knees, a deep sobbing choking up explosively from way down inside of me. The brandy, the high altitude and the strange, incredible knowledge that our long trek was over. I realized that beside me Don too was sobbing his heart out.

The Australian took the brandy away.

"Poor bastards," he said and left us to it.

Hours later, the engines were throttled back and we glided smoothly down at Broome, the landing port for Darwin. On the slipway a staff car was awaiting for us, and two Australian Army officers, staring at our skinny bodies—bare except for loincloths—our blackened skins and our thick matted beards, produced a greatcoat for each of us, and we were driven rapidly away to Army Headquarters.

We barely had a chance to thank the crew of the flying boat.

The first luxury offered us by civilization was a hot bath, and in the tall mirror of the bathroom I saw myself naked for the first time in six months. I was like an undernourished Australian aborigine. My skin was burnt almost jet black, except where the loincloth had left a well-defined white belt around my middle; but the black skin was lightened here and there by festering scars, legacies from the barbed wire at Pasir Panjang, from the cuts of the interrogating officer's sword, and from the tears and scratches of jungle grass and thorns. With a borrowed pair of scissors we hacked off the worst of our beards and hair; then followed the agony of shaving, and afterward the sensuous smoothness of clean-shaven chins. The Australians worked on us with slick efficiency. An equipment officer came into the double room that had been allocated to Don and me, and after giving us underclothes, took my measurements for a uniform and Don's for a civilian suit. No sooner had he finished, than the medical officer paid us a visit and gave us each a complete overhaul. Rather to my surprise he said there was nothing wrong with us that time and good food would not eventually cure. But he warned us that for the first few weeks we should take things easy and eat little but often. He was, strangely enough, worried most by my feet, on the soles of which the skin had grown into a hard pelt. I had to soak them in boiling water, and under a local anesthetic he peeled most of the leathery skin away. The first meal offered us—no doubt ordered by the MO—consisted of cornflakes, milk, chocolate pudding and cocoa. And then it was bed. Sleep, between clean white sheets, for fifteen glorious hours.

When we awoke my uniform was ready for me, so was Don's suit. The Army authorities commandeered him for a couple of days and when he came back it was to say goodbye.

"Well, this is it, Mac," he said. "I'm off home."

The suddenness of his going jolted me, for since we had touched down on the slipway I had hardly given our parting a thought. But it was of course inevitable.

We shook hands.

"Cheers, Don," I said. "Where's your home?"

"Melbourne." He wrote down the address. "Write me when you get back to Blighty."

And he was gone. The man with whom I had shared the most fantastic six months' ordeal that could perhaps come in anyone's lifetime. Looking back, I realized that not once had we quarrelled, though neither of us had ever hesitated to speak his mind. Each had understood the other's point of view and of all the things I had learned from him, tolerance overshadowed all. Thrown together fortuitously, we had reverted to an almost primeval way of life in a long-drawn struggle for self-preservation. When primitive instincts, without the restraints of civilization, might have hurled us at each other's throat, we had remained friends. Hardly at all had I mentioned the background of my life, my hopes and my fears; not once had he mentioned his. There could not possibly have been two men sharing so much danger for so long who knew about each other both so little and so much.

There is not much more of my story to record except the last, blessed bounty of chance with which I will end. There is little point in writing of the succession of days I spent in Darwin; of the lounging about in the sergeants' mess, drinking beer and feeling oddly remote from the others; of the queer, confused, lonely emptiness of the life which I had anticipated would be a magnificent return to sanity—was this, I wondered, the life I had endured so much to come back to? Of the frustration from at first being able to find no official news of the fate of the *Wakefield*; of the deeper frustration on being told that the signal I wished to send to the Air Ministry for news of Pat was considered unimportant; or of my linking up with a re-staffed 205 Squadron, only to learn that not one of my old aircrew colleagues had survived.

One day in the sergeants' mess I was glancing through a pile of old and tattered newspapers. Suddenly a headline and its accompanying picture caught my eye. It was in the April issue of the *Overseas Daily Mail*. As though in the most wonderful vision I read the caption:

FOUR BABIES BORN IN SINGAPORE REFUGEE SHIP

and saw beneath it the picture of a young woman holding in her arms a baby; a baby with screwed-up eyes and its shawl stuffed into its mouth. The baby I had never seen, but the woman, without the slightest possibility of doubt, was Pat.

And it then came flooding over that all I had suffered and endured had become suddenly so very much worthwhile.

Like the tying together of ends in a well-constructed novel, there comes, by the strangest coincidence, a postscript to my story.

On returning to England I was reunited with Pat and after several months of convalescent leave returned to duty with the RAF. I was awarded the DCM (Distinguished Conduct Medal), and promotion to squadron-leader followed rapidly; finally I was posted on Counter-Intelligence work to SEAC and after the end of the Far Eastern war I served under Lord Louis Mountbatten on the war crimes tribunal.

In a vast open-air court room the Japanese war criminals were brought one by one to trial. Those sentenced were hanged on the spot. One morning the first case to be heard was that of a Captain Teruchi. The name meant nothing to me; but the face did. It was a heavy, moon-like face, blank and quite expressionless: the face of a man who either possessed no human feelings or found it best to hide those that he had. My hand went up to my own cheek, still scarred from the turning point of his sword. "I shall be seeing you again," he had said five years before, as I had slumped half-unconscious at his feet.

Late that morning Teruchi was sentenced to death, and when in the coolness of the evening the court rose, I went up to Lord Louis.

"Sir," I said, "may I have Teruchi's ceremonial sword?"

"Why?"

I pointed to the scars on my face. "A personal reason, sir."

"All right, McCormac," Lord Louis said. "It's yours."

The sword is locked away in a cupboard now, safe from the inquisitive fingers of our three children; but sometimes when I am alone I will take it out and think of things that cannot easily be forgotten.

If you enjoyed this you'll like ...

If you enjoyed *You'll Die in Singapore*, Monsoon Books has other similar titles which you'll be sure to want to read.

To order copies online, please visit: www.monsoonbooks.com.sg

monsoon

SOLD FOR SILVER

An autobiography of a girl sold into slavery in Southeast Asia

Janet Lim

'I was looked at, criticized, and after much bargaining sold for $250.'

So begins Janet Lim's ordeal as a *mui tsai*, or slave girl, in 1930s Singapore. But this is only the beginning of a remarkable journey, which sees the author freed from child bondage to assume a position of leadership and obtain true happiness in later life.

After gaining her freedom, Janet is educated by missionaries and serves under colonial tutelage as a nurse. Her misfortunes return, however, when Singapore falls to the Japanese in 1942—the ship that she flees Singapore on is bombed and she drifts for days at sea. Rescued by Indonesian fishermen, she is finally captured and imprisoned in Japanese-occupied Sumatra. To avoid becoming a comfort woman, Janet escapes into the jungle villages of west Sumatra but is once again caught, and this time tortured by the Japanese military police and threatened with the firing squad.

ISBN: 978-981-05-1728-1

(Monsoon Books, 2004)

ROGUE RAIDER
The Tale of Captain Lauterbach and the
Singapore Mutiny

Nigel Barley

Rogue Raider is a humorous fictionalised
history set in Singapore and Southeast Asia
during the First World War. The story centres
on a lovable rogue in the form of Captain Julius Lauterbach of the
German Imperial Navy and the ship that catapulted Lauterbach to
accidental fame (and infamy), His Imperial Majesty's *Emden*.

For every austere virtue of the *Emden*'s noble, ruthless and
gentlemanly commander Lieutenant-Commander Karl von Mueller,
it seems Lauterbach possessed the corresponding vice. He was a beer-
guzzling, cigar-smoking filcher, a braggart and, above all, a survivor.
The Flashmanesque Lauterbach was more interested in making money,
hoarding the spoils of war and womanising than actually fighting in
the war. Imprisoned in Singapore by the British, he instigated the
Singapore Mutiny among his Indian guards as a diversion and made
his escape. The book follows his adventures and subsequent flight
from the British through Asia to America and back to Germany.

ISBN: 978-981-05-5949-6

(Monsoon Books, 2006)

INDISCREET MEMORIES

1901 Singapore through the eyes
of a colonial Englishman

Edwin A. Brown

Stepping off the SS *Hamburg* on a moonlit night in January 1901, Edwin A. Brown knew little about his new home—the Straits Settlement of Singapore. Through diary extracts and personal memories, this young Englishman brings to life characters and events in a country few would recognise today.

Life for the early settlers was always eventful. Entertainment came in the form of comic operas, visiting circuses, balls at Government House and socialising at the Tingel Tangel dance hall. There were rickshaw strikes, sightings of a sea serpent in the Singapore harbour, Sunday morning horse rides around the Settlement and tigers causing havoc in Chinatown.

From the death of Queen Victoria and the coronation of King Edward to the decision by Straits-born Chinese to discard their *towchang* (queues), we come to understand how historical events shaped and affected the society of the day. Indiscreet Memories is one man's true account of life in Singapore as it was over a hundred years ago.

ISBN: 978-981-05-8691-1

(Monsoon Books, 2007)

THE ROSE OF SINGAPORE

An Epic Tale of Love, Loss and
Sexual Awakening in 1950s Malaya
and Singapore

Peter Neville

When Aircraftman First Class Peter Saunders
of the Royal Air Force leaves England for the
Far East in 1951, he is only eighteen years of age. His two-and-a-
half-year tour of duty takes him briefly to Hong Kong and Malaya
before being posted as a cook to RAF Changi, Singapore. For an
adventurous young man such as Peter, Singapore in the early 1950s
holds all the promise of the Orient—exotic surroundings, unusual
customs and mesmerising women. Peter soon meets and falls in love
with a local Chinese girl but only later does he learn she is not entirely
what she seems.

The Rose of Singapore is a moving work of fiction about love,
loss and sexual awakening and is based on the true experiences of the
author, Peter Neville. The backdrop is Singapore and Malaya during
the Emergency period—a time of active Communist terrorism as well
as rising nationalism. Neville describes in minute detail daily life at
that time, bringing vividly to life the Singapore and Malaya of old in
this Tanamera-style blockbuster.

ISBN: 978-981-05-1727-4
(Monsoon Books, 2005)

A COMPANY OF PLANTERS

Confessions of a Colonial
Rubber Planter in 1950s Malaya

John Dodd

Through a collection of letters written to his
best friend and father in England, and from
his own personal diary entries, the young
rubber planter John Dodd has bequeathed us a fascinating, and often
hilarious, memoir of life as a colonial rubber planter.

With true stories and confessions that would make even Somerset
Maugham blush, we discover what life was really like for young
colonial planters in late-1950s Malaya. Life was more than just a
series of *stengahs* in the clubhouse, dalliances in the Chinese brothels
of Penang and charming 'pillow dictionaries'—there were strikes,
riots, snakes, plantation fires and deadly ambushes by Communist
terrorists to contend with. Set against the backdrop of the Emergency
period, the rise of nationalism and Malaya's subsequent Independence,
A Company of Planters is a very personal, moving and humorous
account of one man's experiences on the frequently isolated rubber
plantations of colonial Malaya.

ISBN: 978-981-05-7569-4

(Monsoon Books, 2007)

THE BOAT

Singapore Escape

Cannibalism at Sea

Walter Gibson

In 1942 a ship carrying 500 escapees from Japanese-occupied Singapore set sail from Padang for Ceylon. Halfway to safety she was torpedoed and sank. Amidst the horror and confusion, only one lifeboat was launched—a lifeboat built to carry twenty-eight but to which 135 souls now looked to for salvation.

For twenty-six days she drifted across the Indian Ocean. For twenty-six days, cannibalism, murder, heroism and self-sacrifice drifted with her. When the lifeboat finally ran aground on the island of Sipora, only four had survived: two Javanese seamen, a Chinese girl, Doris Lim, and Walter Gibson of the Argyll and Sutherland Highlanders.

The Boat is Walter Gibson's true account of that horrific event. He captures vividly the mental trauma, the physical pain, the decision to kill or be killed but above all, the determination not to die.

ISBN: 978-981-05-8301-9

(Monsoon Books, 2007)